The Great ★ American **CITIZENSHIP** Quiz

CAN YOU PASS YOUR OWN COUNTRY'S CITIZENSHIP TEST?

Solomon M. Skolnick

Walker & Company
New York

First published in the United States of America in 2005
by Walker Publishing Company, Inc.

Published simultaneously in Canada by
Fitzhenry and Whiteside, Markham, Ontario L3R 4T8

For information about permission to reproduce selections from
this book, write to Permissions, Walker & Company,
104 Fifth Avenue, New York, New York 10011.

Library of Congress Cataloging-in-Publication Data
available upon request
ISBN 0-8027-7722-8

Book design by Mary Jane Di Massi

Visit Walker & Company's Web site at www.walkerbooks.com

Printed in the United States of America

10   9   8   7   6   5   4

Contents

••

Introduction

· ·

Citizenship: The status of a citizen with its attendant duties, rights, and privileges. —American Heritage Dictionary

EACH YEAR THE Department of United States Citizenship and Immigration Services helps hundreds of thousands of immigrants become new American citizens. Among the requirements for a would-be citizen is the ability to answer a selection of some core questions about American history and civic responsibility, each of which is reproduced in the pages that follow. Some of the questions are simple ("What are the colors of the flag?" for example) and some are repetitious or crisscross the same ground. But some of them would challenge even the most knowledgeable student of American history. And behind each of them, as you'll see, are fascinating stories and facts about the founding of America and the unique government and society created on these shores.

Just beneath the surface of each answer lie the circumstances of the moment, the actions of the players involved, and the consequences of these actions, both intended and otherwise. On the lighter side, could

William Bradford and Edward Winslow of Plymouth Colony ever have imagined that, more than 380 years after the meal was served, their journals would offer intriguing information on the menu for the first Thanksgiving in America? More significantly, at a time when our system of presidential election is a hot topic of debate, reviewing the thought process of those who designed the Electoral College as part of the Constitution is both inspiring and comforting.

As a free people, we have come down a long and nearly miraculous path. Our freedom has been sustained by several remarkable documents that have stood the test of time—the Declaration of Independence, the Constitution, the Bill of Rights and other amendments to the Constitution, the Emancipation Proclamation—each of which is reproduced in full at the back of this book. At the country's beginning, liberty itself was contradictory: The craftsmen of our freedom, who had shaken off their own masters, could, in fact, own other men, and denied their own mothers, wives, and daughters the right to vote. Yet time and again, the ideals of our best intentions have ultimately overcome the worst of our actions.

So come and take *The Great American Citizenship Quiz*. It will give you a strong sense of where we've come from and an intimation of what we can be.

Many thanks for their work in research and development for this book to Christa Bourg, Lauren Galit, John Boswell, Katy Weisman, and Linda Johns. My sincerest appreciation to my friend and editor, George Gibson, for his flexibility and stamina. Love and thanks to my wife, Linda, and our children Sophia and Jesse for tolerating odd hours, strange questions, and sometimes unending discussions about historical arcana when there were surely other things they would rather have been doing.

THE QUESTIONS AND answers are reproduced exactly as they appear in the "Samples of U.S. History and Government Questions with Answers" provided by the United States Citizenship and Immigration Services (but not in the same order), revised and modified in August 2004. The wording of some of their answers differs from the text of certain historical documents, such as the Bill of Rights.

THE QUIZ

1 **What is the name of the ship that brought the Pilgrims to America?**

☞ *The* Mayflower

2 **Why did the Pilgrims come to America?**

☞ *For religious freedom*

THE PASSENGERS ON the *Mayflower* referred to themselves collectively as *Oldcomers*. Those who had separated from the Church of England and were leaving religious persecution were known as Saints and the others were known as Strangers. The Leiden group (Saints) included religious separatists who had fled to Holland in 1608 and those who had subsequently joined their church. The London group, some of whom had relatives from Leiden, was primarily associated with the investors in the company funding the voyage.

THE *MAYFLOWER*, WHICH had previously been in service as a merchant ship calling on ports in France and Spain, made two attempts at a transatlantic voyage in the summer of 1620 in tandem with the *Speedwell*. Leaks aboard the *Speedwell* caused the ships to return to England both times. The *Mayflower* departed Plymouth, England, alone on September 6, 1620, with 102 passengers (three of whom were pregnant women), and a crew of about thirty. The Pilgrims explored the shores of Cape Cod Bay but settled, on December 21, 1620, on the mainland inside of what they renamed Plymouth harbor.

OVER THE PAST four centuries the genealogical claim that "My family came on the *Mayflower*" was meant not only to indicate early arrival on these shores but to connote an air of superiority over those whose families had come to America more recently.

CAN YOU FIND an ancestor on this definitive *Mayflower* passenger list? John Alden, Issac Allerton, Mary Allerton (wife), Bartholomew Allerton (son), Mary Allerton (daughter), Remember Allerton (daughter), Don Allerton (no relation to the other Allertons), Don Billington, Eleanor Billington(wife), Frances Billington (relation unknown), John Billington (son), William Bradford, Dorothy May Bradford (wife), William Brewster, Mary Brewster (wife), Love Brewster (son), Wrestling Brewster (son), Richard Britteridge, Peter

Brown, William Butten, Robert Cartier, John Carver, Katherine Carver (wife), James Chilton, Susanna Chilton (wife), Mary Chilton (relation unknown), Richard Clarke, Francis Cooke, John Cooke (son), Humility Cooper, John Crackston, John Crackston (son), Edward Doty, Francis Eaton, Sarah Eaton (wife), Samuel Eaton (son), [first name unknown] Ely (sailor), Thomas English, Moses Fletcher, Edward Fuller, Ann Fuller (wife), Samuel Fuller (son), Samuel Fuller (not related, physician), Richard Gardiner, John Goodman, William Holbeck, John Hooke, Steven Hopkins, Elizabeth Hopkins (wife), Giles Hopkins (son), Constance Hopkins (daughter), Damaris Hopkins (daughter), Oceanis Hopkins (son) (born during voyage), John Howland, John Langmore, William Latham, Edward Leiste, Edmund Margeson, Christopher Martin, Marie Martin, Desire Minter, Elinor More, Jasper More, Richard More, Mary More, William Mullins, Alice Mullins (wife), Joseph Mullins (son), Priscilla Mullins (daughter), Degory Priest, Solomon Prower, John Rigdale, Alice Rigdale, Thomas Rogers, Joseph Rogers (son), Henry Sampson, George Soule, Miles Standish, Rose Standish (wife), Elias Story, Edward Thompson, Edward Tilley, Agnes Tilley (wife), John Tilley, Joan Tilley (John's wife), Elizabeth Tilley (daughter), Thomas Tinker, [the wife of Thomas Tinker, name unknown], [the son of Thomas Tinker, name unknown], William Trevore, John Turner, [two sons of John Turner, names unknown],

Master Richard Warren, William White, Susana White (wife), Peregrine White (son), Resolved White (son), Roger Wilder, Thomas Williams, Edward Winslow, Elizabeth Winslow (wife), and Gilbert Winslow (brother)

3 Who helped the Pilgrims in America?

 The American Indians

THE HOMELAND OF the Wampanoag Indians ("Eastern People" or "People of the First Light") included present-day southeastern Massachusetts between the eastern shore of Narragansett Bay in Rhode Island and the western end of Cape Cod, including Martha's Vineyard and Nantucket.

IN MARCH 1621, Samoset, an Abenaki Indian, walked into the Plymouth settlement and, much to the surprise of the settlers, called out in English, "Welcome." He had learned English from men on fishing boats and later brought Squanto, an Indian who not only spoke English but had been to England. Squanto had been taken to England by Captain George Weymouth and he was later kidnapped and taken to Spain. Squanto returned to his homeland around 1619. During 1621–22 Squanto lived among the Pilgrims in Plymouth and is credited with having taught them much about farming and local fishing. Squanto died at Plymouth in 1622.

HOBBAMOCK, A COUNSELOR to Massasoit, the sachem, or spiritual leader, of the Pokanoket Indians, settled in Plymouth with his family in 1621. He served as a guide and interpreter for the colonists until his death in 1641.

4 What holiday was celebrated for the first time by the American colonists?

· ·

☞ *Thanksgiving*

· ·

THE FIRST NEW ENGLAND Thanksgiving, the antecedent of our current celebration, took place in 1621 at

Plymouth, Massachusetts. However, among the first documented Thanksgivings in America was a religious holiday invoked on December 4, 1619, by English settlers at Berkeley Plantation, near what is now Charles City, Virginia. The group's charter required that their day of arrival be observed yearly as a day of thanksgiving. This plantation would later be the birthplace of Benjamin Harrison, a signer of the Declaration of Independence, President William Henry Harrison, and President Benjamin Harrison, and the site of the 1862 composition of "Taps," the military signal for lights-out, also played at graveside.

CONTEMPORARY ACCOUNTS (written by William Bradford and Edward Winslow) of the three-day Thanksgiving celebration and meal of 1621 in Plymouth state that it included five deer, a large number of turkeys and waterfowl, cod, bass, and the fruit of the harvest. There are conflicting allusions to Thanksgiving celebrations in subsequent years, suggesting that similar occasions were celebrated but not on a regular basis or on a set date.

PRESIDENT WASHINGTON PROCLAIMED Thursday, November 26, 1789, as the first national day of Thanksgiving. For many years afterward, however, there was no regular national observance of Thanksgiving. Twelve years earlier he had, as commander in chief of the Continental forces, issued a general order setting aside Thursday, December 18, 1777, as a day "for Solemn Thanksgiving and Praise."

THANKSGIVING WAS CELEBRATED on the last Thursday of November until 1939 when President Franklin D. Roosevelt moved it one week earlier, responding to pressure from the National Retail Dry Goods Association to aid business by lengthening the shopping period before Christmas. The matter of when to celebrate Thanksgiving was settled in 1941, when Congress passed legislation that the fourth Thursday of November would be observed as a federal holiday beginning in 1942.

IN 1947 PRESIDENT Harry S. Truman "pardoned" a turkey the day before it was scheduled to be served at

★ In 1863, President Abraham Lincoln proclaimed the last Thursday of November as "a day of thanksgiving and praise to our beneficent Father." Sarah Hale, the editor of *Boston Ladies' Magazine* and *Godey's Lady's Book*, was particularly pleased with President Lincoln's Thanksgiving Proclamation. She had led a spirited campaign for many years for the creation of a national day of gratitude to God. Hale was a woman of accomplishment. Her novel, *Northwood; A New England Tale*, included slavery in the plot prior to the publication of *Uncle Tom's Cabin*. Mrs. Hale was also the author of the kindergarten standard "Mary Had a Little Lamb."

the White House Thanksgiving dinner. The pardoning of one fortunate bird is now an annual tradition at the White House.

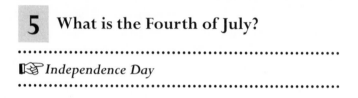

5 **What is the Fourth of July?**

☞ *Independence Day*

6 **What is the date of Independence Day?**

☞ *July 4, 1776*

7 **When was the Declaration of Independence adopted?**

☞ *July 4, 1776*

ON MAY 15, 1776, the Virginia Convention passed a resolution that "the delegates appointed to represent this colony in General Congress be instructed to propose to that respectable body to declare the United Colonies free and independent states." It was in the spirit of that directive that on June 7, 1776, Richard Henry Lee, a delegate from Virginia, read a resolution before the Continental Congress "that these United Colonies are, and of right ought to be, free and independent States, that they are absolved from all allegiance to the British Crown, and that all political connection between them and the State of Great Britain is, and ought to be, totally dissolved."

ON JUNE 11, 1776, consideration of Lee's resolution was postponed. Thomas Jefferson, John Adams, Benjamin Franklin, Roger Sherman, and Robert Livingston, known collectively as the Committee of Five, were appointed to draft a statement, incorporating the resolution in presenting the colonies' case for independence.

ON JULY 2, 1776, the Declaration with the Lee resolution was adopted by twelve of the thirteen colonies (New York did not vote in favor of it until July 9). Congress made some revisions to it on July 2 and 3, and on the morning of July 4. Although no one actually signed the Declaration of Independence on the afternoon of July 4, it was officially adopted that day, and the Committee of Five took the manuscript copy of the document to John Dunlap, official printer to the Congress.

ON THE MORNING of July 5, the printed copies were sent by Congress to various committees and assemblies, and to the commanders of the Continental troops.

THE FIRST CELEBRATION of independence took place in Philadelphia with the ringing of the Liberty Bell, a parade, and the discharging of cannons on July 8, 1776.

THE DECLARATION WAS signed by most of the members of Congress on August 2. George Wythe signed on August 27. On September 4, Richard Henry Lee, Elbridge Gerry, and Oliver Wolcott signed. Matthew

⭐ Key events have often been planned to coincide with Independence Day, such as: the opening of the U.S. Military Academy at West Point (July 4, 1802); the announcement of the Louisiana Purchase (1803); the commencement of construction for the Erie Canal (1817); the beginning of construction for the Baltimore & Ohio railroad in Baltimore, the nation's second largest city in 1818; the laying of the cornerstone of the Washington Monument (1850); the first American International Exposition in Philadelphia (1876); and President Harry S. Truman's declaration of independence for the Philippines (1946). Some unplanned events of note also occurred on July 4, including the death of John Adams (our second president) and Thomas Jefferson (our third president) in 1826 within hours of each other on the fiftieth anniversary of Independence Day; the death of James Monroe (our fifth president), in 1831; and the birth of Calvin Coolidge (our thirtieth president) in 1872.

Thornton signed on November 19, and Thomas McKean sometime after January 1777. Fifty-six men ultimately put their name to parchment.

JULY 4, INDEPENDENCE Day, was declared a federal holiday by Congress in 1941, during World War II.

8 Who was the main writer of the Declaration of Independence?

••

☞ *Thomas Jefferson*

••

(See Appendix A, page 127, for the complete text of the July 4, 1776, published version of the Declaration of Independence.)

IN MAY 1775, after the clashes at Lexington and Concord, Massachusetts, the Second Continental Congress, made up of delegates from twelve colonies (Georgia's delegation arrived in the autumn), convened in Philadelphia. Among its other duties, a committee was convened to draft a Declaration of Independence from Great Britain. Thomas Jefferson, who was perceived to have a "masterly pen," was asked to draft the initial version of the document. His rough draft of the Declaration, with eighty-six emendations by John Adams and Benjamin Franklin, is the document that was adopted by the Continental Congress; printed by John Dunlap, official printer to the Congress; and is in the safekeeping of the manuscript division of the Library of Congress. There are twenty-five known copies of the Dunlap-printed version, including seven in the hands of private owners.

JEFFERSON WAS INITIALLY reluctant to assume the position of author of the Declaration, believing that fellow committee member John Adams was better qualified. But Adams convinced him otherwise, saying, "Reason first: You are a Virginian, and Virginia ought to appear at the head of this business. Reason second: I am obnoxious, suspected and unpopular; you are very much otherwise. Reason third: You can write 10 times better than I can."

THE POLITICAL PHILOSOPHY of the Declaration was not new: It drew key ideas and ideals from the works of British political philosopher John Locke, Continental philosophers, and the Virginia Declaration of Rights, but Jefferson's writing encapsulated these ideas into "self-evident truths" and set down a list of grievances against the king in order to justify to the world the breaking of ties between the colonies and Great Britain.

JEFFERSON'S ORIGINAL DRAFT included a denunciation of the slave trade, which was later edited out by the

Continental Congress. (Ironically, Jefferson himself was a slaveowner). John Adams, writing to Timothy Pickering in 1822, speculated: "I have long wondered that the original draft had not been published. I suppose the reason is the vehement philippic against Negro slavery."

9 What is the basic belief of the Declaration of Independence?

··

☞ *That all men are created equal*

··

THE FOUR IDEALS, also known as self-evident truths, extolled in the Declaration are: equality, natural rights, consent of the governed, and the right to revolution.

America is the only nation in the world that is founded on a creed. Other nations find their identity and cohesion in ethnicity, or geography, or partisan ideology, or cultural tradition. But America was founded on certain ideas—ideas about freedom, about human dignity, and about social responsibility.

—G. K. Chesterton, *What I Saw in America*, 1922

Civil liberties emphasizes the liberty of the individual. In many other forms of government the importance of the individual has disappeared. The individual lives for the state. Here in a democracy the government still exists for the individual, but that does not mean that we do not have to watch and that we do not have to examine ourselves to be sure that we preserve the civil liberties for all our people, which are the basis of our democracy.

—Eleanor Roosevelt, "Civil Liberties—
The Individual and the Community,"
an address to the Chicago Civil Liberties
Committee, March 14, 1940

The powers of a government are just and legitimate only if they are authorized powers, that is, if they derive their authority from the consent of the governed, for they can gain authority in no other way. The reason is the people's right to self-rule; they inherently possess the authority to govern themselves.

—Mortimer J. Adler and William Gorman,
The American Testament, 1975

These are the times that try men's souls. The summer soldier and the sunshine patriot will, in this crisis, shrink from the service of the country; but he that stands it now deserves the love and thanks of man and woman. Tyranny, like hell, is not easily conquered, yet we have this consolation with us, that the harder the conflict the more glorious the triumph. What we obtain too cheap we esteem too lightly; it is dearness only that gives everything its value.

—Thomas Paine, *Common Sense*, 1776

Among the natural rights of the colonists are these: First a right to life, secondly to liberty, thirdly to property; together with the right to defend them in the best manner they can.

—Samuel Adams, "Statement of the Rights of Colonists," 1772

10 **From whom did the United States gain independence as a result of the Revolutionary War?**

☞ *Great Britain*

11 **What country did we fight during the Revolutionary War?**

☞ *Great Britain*

THE FIRST CASUALTY associated with the American Revolutionary War was that of a black man (perhaps an escaped slave) named Crispus Attucks. He was among the five men who died during, or as a result of, the Boston Massacre on March 5, 1770. A color print of that night's events, titled "The Bloody Massacre perpetrated in King Street," which circulated a few weeks later, was a key document in encouraging anti-English sentiment. The artist-engraver of this milestone print was a Boston artisan named Paul Revere.

WE OFTEN THINK that the rebellious colonists moved inexorably toward an all-out war with the Crown, from the Battles of Lexington and Concord and the mobilization of more than thirteen thousand militia in April 1775 to the major engagement at the Battle of Bunker (Breeds) Hill. However, on July 5, 1775, the Continental Congress actually adopted the Olive Branch Petition, appealing directly to King George III for reconciliation. His Majesty refused to look at the petition and further pushed the colonists away by issuing a proclamation declaring the Americans to be in a state of open rebellion.

ALTHOUGH THE AMERICAN Revolution was a popular cause, not all colonials supported a break with England. Approximately five hundred thousand whites (20 percent of that population) were loyalists, or "Tories," who did not necessarily agree with British policies, such as the Stamp Act, but felt that peaceful means were the appropriate remedy.

THE FIRST MAJOR American victory in the Revolutionary War did not come until October 7, 1777 (fifteen months after the Declaration of Independence), at the Battle of Saratoga, New York. Ten days later General John Burgoyne and his army of fifty-seven hundred men surrendered to the Americans led by General Horatio Gates. The British prisoners were marched to Boston, placed on ships, and sent back to England after swearing not to serve again in the war. News of the American victory at Saratoga traveled to Europe, after which Benjamin Franklin was received by the French Royal Court.

THE FRENCH PLAYED a decisive role in the colonists' ability to defeat the British. In February 1778, America and France signed a Treaty of Amity and Commerce, in which France recognized America and offered trade concessions. The two nations also entered into a Treaty of Alliance, which stipulated that if France entered the war, neither country would lay down its arms until America won its independence, that neither would conclude peace with Britain without the consent of the other, and that each guaranteed the other's possessions in America.

THE AMERICAN REVOLUTION effectively ended with the surrender of the British under Lord Charles Cornwallis at Yorktown, Virginia, on October 19, 1781. However, British troops continued to hold New York City for two more years until they finally departed on November 25, 1783.

12 Who said, "Give me liberty or give me death"?

••

☞ *Patrick Henry*

••

THE INVOCATION TO "Give me liberty or give me death" concluded a speech on March 23, 1775, at a meeting of the Virginia Legislature, also known as the House of Burgesses. Patrick Henry was urging his fellow Virginians to arm themselves in self-defense against what he perceived to be increasingly oppressive rule by the British Crown. Less than a month later, Henry would take a lead role in a confrontation with Lord Dunmore, the royal governor of Virginia, over Dunmore's seizure, without just compensation, of gunpowder from the local militia.

PATRICK HENRY HAD been a member of the House of Burgesses in 1765 at the time of the Stamp Act. He offered resolutions declaring the exclusive right of the

Memorable quotes from the revolutionary era:

Let justice be done though the heavens should fall.

—John Adams, in a letter to Count Sarsfield, February 3, 1776

We must all hang together, or assuredly we shall all hang separately.

—Benjamin Franklin, July 4, 1776

There! His Majesty can now read my name without glasses. And he can double the reward on my head!

—John Hancock, signing the Declaration of Independence

The hour is fast approaching, on which the Honor and Success of this army, and the safety of our bleeding Country depend. Remember, officers and Soldiers, that you are free men, fighting for the blessings of Liberty—that slavery will be your portion, and that of your posterity, if you do not acquit yourselves like men.

—George Washington, general orders, August 23, 1776

Men who content themselves with the semblance of truth and a display of words talk much of our obligations to Great Britain for protection. Had she a single eye to our advantage? A nation of shopkeepers are seldom so disinterested.

—Samuel Adams, speech at the Pennsylvania State House, August 1, 1776 colonists, as Englishmen, to tax themselves, and made stirring speeches against the Act. His stance was seen as "revolutionary" and bordering on treason more than a decade before the Declaration of Independence.

IN 1787 HENRY voted against adopting the Constitution because he felt that it created a central government that was too powerful. He believed that the individual states in the United States should govern themselves with a weak central government behind them.

13 What were the names of the thirteen original states?

....

☞ *New Hampshire, Massachusetts, Rhode Island, Connecticut, New York, New Jersey, Pennsylvania, Delaware, Maryland, Virginia, North Carolina, South Carolina, and Georgia*

....

14 What were the thirteen original states of the United States called?

....

☞ *Colonies*

....

Colony	Year Founded	Founded By
Virginia	1607	London Company
Massachusetts	1620	Massachusetts Bay Company
Maryland	1634	Lord Baltimore
Connecticut	c. 1635	Thomas Hooker
Rhode Island	1636	Roger Williams
Delaware	1638	Peter Minuit and the New Sweden Company
New Hampshire	1638	John Wheelwright
North Carolina	1653	Virginians
South Carolina	1663	Eight nobles with a royal charter from Charles II
New Jersey	1664	Lord Berkeley and Sir George Carteret
New York	1664	Duke of York
Pennsylvania	1681	William Penn
Georgia	1732	James Edward Oglethorpe

15 What are the colors of the flag?

☞ *Red, white, and blue*

ALTHOUGH THERE IS no documentary evidence enumerating the reasons for the colors of the American flag, a report by Charles Thompson, secretary of the Continental Congress, specified the meaning of the colors of the *seal* of the United States:

> The colors of the pales (the vertical stripes) are those used in the flag of the United States of America; White signifies purity and innocence, Red, hardiness & valour, and Blue, the color of the Chief (the broad band above the stripes) signifies vigilance, perseverance & justice.

16 How many stars are there in our flag?

☞ *Fifty*

17 What color are the stars on our flag?

☞ *White*

18 What do the stars on the flag mean?

☞ *One for each state in the Union*

19 How many stripes are there in the flag?

☞ *Thirteen*

20 What color are the stripes?

☞ *Red and white*

21 What do the stripes on the flag mean?

☞ *They represent the original thirteen states*

ON JUNE 14, 1777, the Continental Congress passed the first Flag Act: "Resolved, That the flag of the United States be made of thirteen stripes, alternate red and white; that the union be thirteen stars, white in a blue field, representing a new Constellation." George Washington (1789–94) was the only president to serve under this initial version of the flag.

THE LOVELY STORY that almost every schoolchild was told about Betsy Ross is just that, a story. As we learned,

General George Washington, accompanied by two members of Congress, visited Mrs. Ross in her home and asked that she create a flag from a drawing that they had brought. At her suggestion, General Washington made revisions in the design. When they returned, she presented them with the completed Stars and Stripes. However, this version of the story was first published by a grandson of Mrs. Ross in 1870, more than ninety years after the "fact," which has never been borne out by historical evidence.

FRANCIS HOPKINSON, a signer of the Declaration of Independence, a lawyer, a congressman from New Jersey, a poet, an artist, and a civil servant with a distinguished career (according to the journals of the Continental Congress), is a good candidate as the designer of the first Stars and Stripes. Payment for his work (which he ultimately failed to receive due to an odd series of events concerning his actual role in the design, and political enmity) was to be a "quarter cask of the public wine."

THE FIFTEEN-STAR, fifteen-stripe flag was authorized by the Flag Act of January 13, 1794, adding two stripes and two stars for the new states of Vermont and Kentucky. The regulation went into effect on May 1, 1795. This was the only U.S. flag to have more than thirteen stripes. It flew during the bombardment of Fort McHenry, September 13, 1814, during the War of 1812, when Francis Scott Key wrote the poem that became the lyrics for "The Star-Spangled Banner." The five presidents who served under this flag were George Washington (1794–97), John Adams (1797–1801), Thomas Jefferson (1801–9), James Madison (1809–17), and James Monroe (1817–25).

THE FLAG ACT of April 4, 1818, provided for a return to the thirteen-stripe design and designated that one star symbolize each state, a new one to be added to the flag on the Fourth of July following the admission of each new state.

AN EXECUTIVE ORDER of President William Howard Taft, dated June 24, 1912, established the official proportions of the elements of the flag and provided for arrangement of the stars in six horizontal rows of eight each, to accommodate the statehood of New Mexico and Arizona, as the forty-seventh and forty-eighth states, a single point of each star to be facing upward.

BY AN EXECUTIVE order of President Dwight D. Eisenhower, dated January 3, 1959, a forty-ninth star was added to the flag in honor of the statehood of Alaska, and the arrangement of the stars was shifted to seven rows of seven stars each, staggered horizontally and vertically.

ANOTHER EXECUTIVE ORDER of President Eisenhower's, dated August 21, 1959, provided for a fiftieth star to

⭐ The U.S. Army and Navy have a traditional way of folding the flag into the shape of a tricornered hat, emblematic of the hats worn by colonial soldiers during the war for independence. The red and white stripes are folded under so that all that can be seen is a triangle of blue with several stars. When a flag is so worn out that it is no longer fit to serve as a symbol of our country, it should be destroyed by burning in a dignified manner. Many American Legion posts regularly conduct a dignified flag-burning ceremony, often on Flag Day, June 14.

celebrate the statehood of Hawaii, with a new arrangement of the stars in nine rows, staggered horizontally, and eleven columns, staggered vertically.

22 What is the national anthem of the United States called?

☞ *"The Star-Spangled Banner"*

23 Who wrote "The Star-Spangled Banner"?

☞ *Francis Scott Key*

DURING THE WAR of 1812, Francis Scott Key and Colonel John Skinner, the government's prisoner of war exchange agent, were sent to negotiate the release of a prisoner named Dr. William Beanes from the British. Key and Skinner unwittingly boarded a British warship in Chesapeake Bay as it was preparing to bombard Fort McHenry in Baltimore. The British agreed to release Dr. Beanes but continued to hold all three Americans until the battle was over. The bombardment began on September 13, 1814, and continued through the night. Key's morning view was obscured by the smoky haze lingering in the aftermath of the battle. At 7:00 a.m., a thinning mist showed that the American flag was still flying over the fort. An ecstatic Key wrote the verses to "The Star-Spangled Banner" and soon thereafter had it published as the "Defense of Fort McHenry." His poem attained wide popularity set to the tune of a British drinking song "To Anacreon in Heaven," which we now know as "The Star-Spangled Banner."

IN 1916, DURING World War I, Woodrow Wilson ordered that "The Star-Spangled Banner" be played at military occasions. In 1918, the song was first played at a baseball game during the World Series between the Boston Red Sox and the Chicago Cubs. A band started an apparently impromptu performance of "The Star-Spangled Banner" during the seventh-inning stretch. The players and fans stood up, took off their hats, and sang. It was adopted as the national anthem of the United States by a congressional resolution on March 3, 1931.

WHAT WE ARE accustomed to singing as "The Star-Spangled Banner" is actually only the first of four verses Key wrote:

Oh, say can you see, by the dawn's early light,
What so proudly we hailed at the twilight's last gleaming?
Whose broad stripes and bright stars, through the perilous fight,
O'er the ramparts we watched, were so gallantly streaming?
And the rockets' red glare, the bombs bursting in air,
Gave proof through the night that our flag was still there.
O say, does that star-spangled banner yet wave
O'er the land of the free and the home of the brave?

On the shore, dimly seen through the mists of the deep,
Where the foe's haughty host in dread silence reposes,
What is that which the breeze, o'er the towering steep,
As it fitfully blows, now conceals, now discloses?
Now it catches the gleam of the morning's first beam,
In full glory reflected now shines on the stream:
'Tis the star-spangled banner! O long may it wave
O'er the land of the free and the home of the brave.

And where is that band who so vauntingly swore
That the havoc of war and the battle's confusion
A home and a country should leave us no more?
Their blood has wiped out their foul footstep's pollution.
No refuge could save the hireling and slave
From the terror of flight, or the gloom of the grave:

And the star-spangled banner in triumph doth wave
O'er the land of the free and the home of the brave.

Oh! thus be it ever, when freemen shall stand
Between their loved homes and the war's desolation!
Blest with victory and peace, may the heaven-rescued land
Praise the Power that hath made and preserved us a nation.
Then conquer we must, for our cause it is just,
And this be our motto: "In God is our trust."
And the star-spangled banner forever shall wave
O'er the land of the free and the home of the brave!

TITLE 36, CHAPTER 10, of the U.S. Code* states that

> During rendition of the national anthem when the
> flag is displayed, all present except those in uniform
> should stand at attention facing the flag with the
> right hand over the heart. Men not in uniform
> should remove their headdress with their right hand
> and hold it at the left shoulder, the hand being over
> the heart. Persons in uniform should render the
> military salute at the first note of the anthem and
> retain this position until the last note. When the flag

---

*The U.S. Code is the codification by subject matter of the general and perma-
nent laws of the United States. It is divided by broad subjects into fifty titles
and published by the Office of the Law Revision Counsel of the U.S. House of
Representatives. Since 1926, the U.S. Code has been published every six years.
In between editions, annual cumulative supplements are published in order to
present the most current information.

is not displayed, those present should face toward the music and act in the same manner they would if the flag were displayed there.

THERE WAS AN unsuccessful movement during the administration of President John F. Kennedy in the early 1960s to make "America the Beautiful" a co–national anthem with "The Star-Spangled Banner."

"STARS AND STRIPES Forever," a patriotic American marching song composed by John Philip Sousa in 1896, was designated by Congress as the national march of the United States of America.

24 How many states are there in the Union (the United States)?

☞ *Fifty*

25 What are the forty-ninth and fiftieth states of the Union?

☞ *Alaska and Hawaii*

THE STATES WERE admitted to the Union in the following order: 1. Delaware (December 7, 1787) 2. Pennsylvania (December 12, 1787) 3. New Jersey (December 18, 1787) 4. Georgia (January 2, 1788) 5. Connecticut (January 9, 1788) 6. Massachusetts (February 6, 1788) 7. Maryland (April 28, 1788) 8. South Carolina (May 23, 1788) 9. New Hampshire (June 21, 1788) 10. Virginia (June 25, 1788) 11. New York (July 26, 1788) 12. North Carolina (November 21, 1789) 13. Rhode Island (May 29, 1790) 14. Vermont (March 4, 1791) 15. Kentucky (June 1, 1792) 16. Tennessee (June 1, 1796) 17. Ohio (March 1, 1803) 18. Louisiana (April 30, 1812) 19. Indiana (December 11, 1816) 20. Mississippi (December 10, 1817) 21. Illinois (December 3, 1818) 22. Alabama (December 14, 1819) 23. Maine (March 15, 1820) 24. Missouri (August 10, 1821) 25. Arkansas (June 15, 1836) 26. Michigan (January 26, 1837) 27. Florida (March 3, 1845) 28. Texas (December 29, 1845) 29. Iowa (December 28, 1846) 30. Wisconsin (May 29, 1848) 31. California (September 9, 1850) 32. Minnesota (May 11, 1858) 33. Oregon (February 14, 1859) 34. Kansas (January 29, 1861) 35. West Virginia (June 20, 1863) 36. Nevada (October 31, 1864) 37. Nebraska (March 1, 1867) 38. Colorado (August 1, 1876) 39. North Dakota (November 2, 1889) 40. South Dakota (November 2, 1889) 41. Montana (November 8, 1889) 42. Washington (November 11, 1889) 43. Idaho (July 3, 1890) 44. Wyoming (July 10, 1890) 45. Utah (January 4, 1896) 46. Oklahoma (November

16, 1907) 47. New Mexico (January 6, 1912) 48. Arizona (February 14, 1912) 49. Alaska (January 3, 1959) 50. Hawaii (August 21, 1959).

ARTICLE IV, SECTION 3, of the Constitution provides for the inclusion of new states but stipulates that the new state may not be formed from within an existing state or by the joining of two or more states without the consent of the legislature of the state(s) involved and of the Congress.

EACH OF THE fifty states is divided into smaller jurisdictions called counties, except in Alaska where they are called boroughs, and Louisiana in which they are called parishes.

BETWEEN DECEMBER 20, 1860, and June 8, 1861, eleven states seceded from the Union to form the Confederate States of America. South Carolina, Mississippi, Florida, and Alabama seceded while James Buchanan was still in office, though Abraham Lincoln had won the election. Georgia, Louisiana, Texas, Virginia, Arkansas, North Carolina, and Tennessee seceded after Lincoln took office, precipitating the Civil War (1861–65). All eleven states were readmitted to the Union between June 1868 and July 1870 during the presidencies of Andrew Johnson and Ulysses S. Grant.

26 Which president is called the "Father of his country"?

☞ *George Washington*

GEORGE WASHINGTON WAS born in Westmoreland County, Virginia, on February 22, 1732. He was a surveyor, a British officer in the French and Indian War (1754–60), a member of the House of Burgesses, and a member of both the First (1774) and the Second (1775) Continental Congresses. In 1774 Washington coauthored with George Mason the Fairfax County Resolves, which protested the British "Intolerable Acts"—legislation passed by the British to punish the colonies in the wake of the December 16, 1773, Boston Tea Party. During the Revolutionary War, he was named the commander in chief of the Continental Army, having been nominated for that post by John Adams, who believed Washington was the one man who could unify the Northern and Southern colonies in the struggle for independence. He was the first president of the United States, serving from 1789 to 1797.

THE FATHER OF our country had no biological children of his own, although he did become stepfather to the two children of his wife, the widow Martha Dandridge Custis, from her previous marriage.

⭐ Many places are named after George Washington, including the nation's capital, a state, thirty-one counties, and seventeen communities.

GOUVERNEUR MORRIS, IN his eulogy of Washington on his death in 1799, remarked: "Born to high destinies, he was fashioned for them by the hand of nature. His form was noble—his port majestic. On his front were enthroned the virtues which exalt, and those which adorn the human character. So dignified his deportment, no man could approach him but with respect—none was great in his presence. You have all seen him, and you all have felt the reverence he inspired. . . ."

WASHINGTON DID NOT lead a public fight against slavery because he believed it would tear the new nation apart. Privately, however, Washington arranged for all the slaves he owned to be freed after the death of his wife, and he left instructions for the continued care and education of some of his former slaves and their children.

27 What is the executive branch of our government?

· ·

••

28 Who was the first president of the United States?

••

☞ *George Washington*

••

GEORGE WASHINGTON WAS made president in 1789 by a unanimous vote of the electors, and took the oath of office on April 30 at Federal Hall in New York City, the nation's first capital. He had to borrow money to repay debts and pay for his trip from Virginia to New York. He served two full four-year terms through 1797.

WASHINGTON HAD A clear sense that he, and his peers, were laying a cornerstone for the future. He wrote to James Madison: "As the first of every thing in our situation will serve to establish a Precedent it is devoutly wished on my part, that these precedents may be fixed on true principles."

"I DO SOLEMNLY swear (or affirm) that I will faithfully execute the Office of President of the United States, and will to the best of my ability, preserve, protect and defend the Constitution of the United States." This oath of office, taken by George Washington on April 30, 1789, has remained the same for more than 225 years. (Executive Oath of Office, Constitution of the United States, Article II, Section 1, clause 8)

WASHINGTON INSISTED ON his power to act independently of Congress in foreign conflicts. He issued a Declaration of Neutrality in 1793 on his own authority in the conflict between England and France. He also acted to put down a rebellion (the Whiskey Rebellion of 1794) by farmers in western Pennsylvania who protested a federal whiskey tax.

THE NATION'S CAPITAL was located in Philadelphia during Washington's administration, making him the only president who didn't live in Washington, D.C., during his presidency.

WASHINGTON REFUSED THE presidential salary of $25,000, a huge sum in 1789. The president's salary was increased by Congress to $50,000 in 1873, $75,000 in 1909, $100,000 in 1949, $200,000 in 1969, and $400,000 in 2001. Traditionally, the president is the highest-paid government employee, which helps set a cap on federal salaries.

WASHINGTON'S REFUSAL TO accept a crown and his willingness to relinquish the office after two terms established the precedents for limits on the power of the presidency.

GEORGE WASHINGTON WAS the first of eight presidents to be born as British subjects before the United States was a country. The others were John Adams, Thomas Jefferson, James Madison, James Monroe, John Quincy Adams, Andrew Jackson, and William Henry Harrison. Martin Van Buren was the first president to be born a U.S. citizen.

GEORGE WASHINGTON WAS the first of six presidents who were slaveowners. The others were Thomas Jefferson, James Madison, Andrew Jackson, James Polk, and Zachary Taylor.

29 In what month do we vote for the president?

••
☞ *November*
••

NATIONAL ELECTIONS ARE held on the Tuesday after the first Monday in November, in accordance with a law passed by Congress in 1845 establishing the first uniform Election Day. The law guaranteed the simultaneous selection of the electors in all states. Prior to this law, elections could be held on different days and dates in each state provided that they completed the selection of their electors anytime within a thirty-four-day period before the first Wednesday of December. November was chosen because it was felt that harvest time (in the largely agrarian United States of the time) would be over and men would be able to travel to their polling places. Tuesday was chosen to give voters time to travel on Monday since Sunday was generally a day for church attendance.

30 In what month is the new president inaugurated?

☞ *January*

THE CONSTITUTION ESTABLISHED March 4 as Inauguration Day in order to allow sufficient time for officials to gather and count election returns by hand and for newly elected officeholders to travel to the capital. When March 4 fell on a Sunday, as it did in 1821, 1849, 1877, and 1917, the ceremonies were held on March 5.

GEORGE WASHINGTON'S FIRST inauguration did not take place until April 30, 1789. Although it was scheduled for March 4, additional time was needed to actually count the ballots, which made it necessary to give the president-elect more time to travel from his home in Mount Vernon, Virginia, to the capital in New York City.

BY THE EARLY part of the twentieth century, modern transportation and communication devices rendered the three-month transition period anachronistic. The Twentieth Amendment to the Constitution, ratified in 1933, moved the inauguration date to January 20. Franklin D. Roosevelt was the last president to be inaugurated on March 4 [1933] and the first president to be inaugurated in January.

CAPTURING AND PUBLICIZING presidential inaugurations:
First inaugural to be photographed: James Buchanan (March 4, 1857)
First inaugural recorded by a movie camera: William McKinley (March 4, 1897)
First inaugural broadcast nationally by radio: Calvin Coolidge (March 4, 1925)
First inaugural recorded by a talking newsreel: Herbert Hoover (March 4, 1929)
First inaugural broadcast live on television: Harry S. Truman (January 20, 1949)
First inaugural to be broadcast live on the Internet: William J. (Bill) Clinton (January 20, 1997)

Some of the most memorable quotes from inaugural addresses:

With malice toward none, with charity for all, with firmness in the right as God gives us to see the right, let us strive on to finish the work we are in, to bind up the nation's wounds, to care for him who shall have borne the battle and for his widow and his orphan, to do all which may achieve and cherish a just and lasting peace among ourselves and with all nations.

—Abraham Lincoln, Second Inaugural Address, March 4, 1865

The only thing we have to fear is fear itself.

—Franklin Delano Roosevelt
First Inaugural Address, March 4, 1933

Ask not what your country can do for you—ask what you can do for your country.

—John F. Kennedy, Inaugural Address, January 20, 1961

31 Who is the president of the United States today?

☞ *George W. Bush*

GEORGE W. BUSH, the forty-third president, is only the second son of a president (George H. W. Bush, the forty-first) to be elected president. John Quincy Adams (the sixth) was the son of John Adams (the second). Benjamin Harrison (the twenty-third) was the grandson of William Henry Harrison (the ninth). George W. Bush was first elected in 2000 (with an electoral majority but not a popular majority) and re-elected in 2004 with more than 51 percent of the popular vote.

THE PRESIDENTS, PRIOR to George W. Bush, were: 1. George Washington (1789–97) 2. John Adams (1797–1801) 3. Thomas Jefferson (1801–09) 4. James Madison (1809–17) 5. James Monroe (1817–25) 6. John Quincy Adams (1825–29) 7. Andrew Jackson (1829–37) 8. Martin Van Buren (1837–41) 9. William Henry Harrison (March 4–April 4, 1841) 10. John Tyler (1841–45) 11. James K. Polk (1845–49) 12. Zachary Taylor (1849–50) 13. Millard Fillmore (1850–53) 14. Franklin Pierce (1853–57) 15. James Buchanan (1857–61) 16. Abraham Lincoln (1861–65) 17. Andrew Johnson (1865–69) 18. Ulysses S. Grant (1869–77) 19. Rutherford B. Hayes (1877–81) 20. James Garfield (March 4–September 19, 1881) 21. Chester A. Arthur (1881–85) 22. Grover Cleveland (1885–89) 23. Benjamin Harrison (1889–93) 24. Grover Cleveland (1893–97) 25. William McKinley (1897–1901) 26. Theodore Roosevelt (1901–09) 27. William Howard Taft (1909–13) 28. Woodrow Wilson (1913–21) 29. Warren G. Harding (1921–23) 30.

Calvin Coolidge (1923–29) 31. Herbert Hoover (1929–33) 32. Franklin D. Roosevelt (1933–45) 33. Harry S. Truman (1945–53) 34. Dwight D. Eisenhower (1953–61) 35. John F. Kennedy (1961–63) 36. Lyndon Baines Johnson (1963–69) 37. Richard M. Nixon (1969–74) 38. Gerald R. Ford (1974–77) 39. Jimmy Carter (1977–81) 40. Ronald Reagan (1981–89) 41. George H. W. Bush (1989–93) 42. William Jefferson (Bill) Clinton (1993–2001).

THE FOLLOWING PRESIDENTS (an abbreviated list) were and are, sometimes very distant, cousins: James Madison and George Washington; James Madison and Zachary Taylor; Grover Cleveland and Ulysses S. Grant; Theodore Roosevelt and Martin Van Buren; Theodore Roosevelt and Franklin D. Roosevelt; Franklin D. Roosevelt and Ulysses S. Grant; Franklin D. Roosevelt and Zachary Taylor; Richard M. Nixon and William Howard Taft; Richard M. Nixon and Herbert Hoover; George H. W. Bush and Franklin Pierce; George H. W. Bush and Theodore Roosevelt; George H. W. Bush and Gerald Ford; and George H. W. Bush and Abraham Lincoln. George H. W. Bush and George W. Bush are (respectively) tenth cousins seven times removed, and eight times removed, of George Washington, through John Spencer Esq., a fifteenth-century ancestor.

32 For how long do we elect the president?

☞ *A four-year term*

33 How many terms can a president serve?

☞ *A president can be elected to two four-year terms. A president can serve up to two years of a predecessor's term and also be elected to two four-year terms.*

UNTIL THE TWENTY-SECOND Amendment to the Constitution was ratified on February 27, 1951, there were no term limits for the president. The two-term maximum was a tradition but not a law. George Washington "retired" after two terms and his early successors were clear about their belief, as articulated by Thomas Jefferson, that "If some termination to the services of the chief Magistrate be not fixed by the Constitution, or supplied by practice, his office, nominally four years, will in fact become for life."

THE TWENTY-SECOND Amendment states that no person may be elected president more than twice. The vice president or another person who succeeds to the presidency, and serves as president or acting president for more than two years, may not be elected president more than once. The maximum length of time one person may serve as president is ten consecutive years. That person would first succeed to the presidency and serve for no more than two years, and then be elected to two full four-year terms. Had Lyndon Baines Johnson, who succeeded John F. Kennedy on his death in November 1963, run and won in 1968 (and completed his term) he would have been president legally for ten years; however he decided not to seek reelection.

ULYSSES S. GRANT (1869–77) sought a third term but was not nominated by his party (the Republicans).

THEODORE ROOSEVELT, HAVING served three-and-a-half years of the term of President William McKinley, following McKinley's assassination in 1901, served four years in his own right (1905–09) and then ran unsuccessfully in 1912.

FRANKLIN D. ROOSEVELT was the only president to be elected more than twice. He died in April 1945 at the beginning of his fourth term in office, having served for more than twelve years. Harry S. Truman, his successor, who was president when the Twenty-second Amendment passed Congress in 1947, was the last president eligible to run for a third term.

34 Which president was the first commander in chief of the U.S. military?

☞ *George Washington*

35 Who is the commander in chief of the U.S. military?

☞ *The president of the United States*

ACCORDING TO THE Constitution (Article II, Section 2), the president "shall be Commander in Chief of the Army and Navy of the United States, and of the Militia of the several States, when called into the actual Service of the United States."

IN 1976 DURING America's bicentennial, George Washington was posthumously promoted to the six-star rank of General of the Armies, the highest military rank ever bestowed upon any American.

TWELVE COMMANDERS IN chief were generals prior to becoming commander in chief: George Washington, William Henry Harrison, Zachary Taylor, Andrew Johnson, Ulysses S. Grant, Rutherford B. Hayes, Benjamin

Harrison, William Henry Harrison, Chester A. Arthur, James Garfield, Franklin Pierce, and Dwight D. Eisenhower.

THE ONLY COMMANDERS in chief who did not serve in the military in any capacity were: John Adams, John Quincy Adams, Martin Van Buren, James K. Polk, Grover Cleveland, William Howard Taft, Woodrow Wilson, Warren G. Harding, Calvin Coolidge, Herbert Hoover, Franklin D. Roosevelt, and William J. (Bill) Clinton.

GROVER CLEVELAND PAID a replacement $300 to fight in his place during the Civil War, which was legal and not unusual at the time among the wealthy.

ULYSSES S. GRANT AND Dwight D. Eisenhower were the only presidents to graduate from the U.S. Military Academy at West Point. President Jimmy Carter was the only president to graduate from the Naval Academy at Annapolis.

36 Who is the vice president of the United States?

 Richard B. Cheney

IN NOVEMBER 2004 Richard B. (Dick) Cheney was elected to his second term as the vice president of President George W. Bush.

THE JOB THAT John Adams, the first vice president, described as "the most insignificant office that ever the invention of man contrived or his imagination conceived" has one constitutionally mandated (Article I, Section 3) duty: to serve as the president of the Senate. The Constitution (Article II, Section 1) also provides for the vice president to take over the duties of the president should the president be incapacitated or die.

FROM 1789 TO 1804 no one ran to become vice president. The candidate with the most electoral votes became president, and the runner-up became vice president. This plan to place the most qualified persons in the top two offices foundered as people of different political persuasions, who had been competing for the same office, often found themselves not working well together at the head of the executive branch of the government. In 1804 Congress passed the Twelfth Amendment to the Constitution, which created the concept of a "ticket" comprising one nominee for president and one for vice president.

IN 1841 JOHN Tyler became the first vice president to succeed a president after a death when he replaced William Henry Harrison, who died after one month in office. (Harrison served the shortest length of time of any president.)

WHAT BETTER WAY to prepare for the office of president than by first serving as vice president? Fourteen men who were vice president have also become president. They were John Adams, Thomas Jefferson, Martin Van Buren, John Tyler, Millard Fillmore, Andrew Johnson, Chester A. Arthur, Theodore Roosevelt, Calvin Coolidge, Harry S. Truman, Lyndon Baines Johnson, Richard M. Nixon, Gerald Ford, and George H. W. Bush.

HOWEVER, PREPARATION DOESN'T always pay off. John Breckenridge, Hubert Humphrey, Walter Mondale, and Al Gore were all vice presidents who received their party's nomination but never became president.

A HISTORY OF vice presidential pay:

1789	$5,000
1873	$10,000
1906	$12,000
1946	$20,000
1949	$30,000
1951	$35,000
1964	$43,000
1969	$62,500
1994	$171,000

2001	$175,400
2003	$198,600
2004	$202,900

⭐ Although the president is limited to two terms in office the vice president can make a career of it; there is no limit to how many times a person can run, or how many years a person can serve, as the nation's most visible understudy.

37 According to the Constitution, a person must meet certain requirements in order to be eligible to become president. Name one of these requirements.

....

☞ *Article II, Section 1, clause 5 of the Constitution requires that the president must meet three requirements:*
(1) Be a natural-born citizen of the United States.
(2) Be at least thirty-five years old.
(3) Have lived in the United States for at least fourteen years.

....

THE FOUNDING FATHERS believed that these criteria would ensure that the man in the office (women could not vote until the ratification of the Nineteenth Amendment of the Constitution in 1920, let alone hold high office) understood the nature of the country and had sufficient life experience to serve it well. The vice president, who sits only a heartbeat away from the presidency, has to meet the same criteria.

THE YOUNGEST ELECTED president was John F. Kennedy at forty-three; the youngest to serve was Theodore Roosevelt, who assumed the office at the age of forty-two after the assassination of William McKinley.

DETRACTORS OF PRESIDENTIAL candidates have occasionally used this constitutional clause for their own political agendas. Unsubstantiated claims were made that Chester A. Arthur was born in Canada, and it was rumored that Andrew Jackson entered the world while on board a ship in international waters.

38 Who elects the president of the United States?

....

 The Electoral College

....

MANY PEOPLE THINK the president is chosen by winning a majority of the popular vote, but that is not strictly the case. The Framers of the Constitution were reluctant to give the people the power to directly elect the president. Some argued that the citizenry was too beholden to local interests, too easily duped by promises; or perhaps a national election, in the preindustrial era, was just impractical. The Framers created a complex process using electors, a group of citizens designated to select the president, which came to be known as the Electoral College. The president is actually chosen by this body (codified in federal law in 1845 as the College of Electors), which is made up of 538 electors from the fifty states and Washington, D.C. The number of electors from each state is equal to the combined representation of that state in the Senate and the House of Representatives. Each state, regardless of its population, has two senators, and a varying number of representatives, based on population.

THE TWELFTH AMENDMENT to the Constitution, ratified in 1804, changed the provisions of Article II relating to presidential elections. Originally, the Electoral College elected both the president and the vice president in a single election; the person with a majority would become president and the runner-up would become vice president. Candidates now form a party ticket with one candidate for president and one for vice president, guaranteeing that the ticket is elected as a whole.

THE TWELFTH AMENDMENT prohibits an elector from voting for a presidential and vice presidential candidate who both reside in the same state as the elector. It does not prohibit the election of a president and vice president from the same state; however, running mates usually come from different states to prevent situations that would cause electors of a state to vote for a candidate from a different party because of residency rules. During the 2000 presidential election, it was alleged that presidential candidate George W. Bush and his running mate Dick Cheney were both residents of Texas. Bush was the governor and a resident of Texas at the time. Cheney had lived, and was registered to vote, in Texas, but a few months before the election he moved his legal residence to Wyoming.

FOUR PRESIDENTS HAVE been elected without a majority (also called a plurality) of popular votes because they garnered a majority of the electoral votes: John Quincy Adams (1824) had 44,000 fewer votes than Andrew Jackson at a time when the electors from six of the then–twenty-four states were chosen by their state legislatures, not by popular vote; Rutherford B. Hayes (1876), whose critics referred to him as "His Fraudulency" and "Rutherfraud," trailed Samuel Tilden by one quarter of a million votes; Benjamin Harrison (1888) had 95,000 fewer votes than Grover Cleveland; and George W. Bush (2000) trailed Al Gore by some five hundred thousand votes.

THE POST–CIVIL WAR Fourteenth Amendment provides that any state official who has engaged in insurrection or rebellion against the United States or given aid and comfort to its enemies is disqualified from serving as an elector.

RESIDENTS OF WASHINGTON, D.C., have often thought of themselves as electoral orphans. There were no electors from our nation's capital until the Twenty-third Amendment to the Constitution was ratified in 1961.

BECAUSE OF THE complexity of the concept and differing opinions about its fairness, the Electoral College has been the subject of more than seven hundred proposals for constitutional amendments, more than on any other issue. However, the system has remained in place since none of these proposals had sufficient support to be passed by Congress.

THE MANNER OF choosing its state's electors is determined by each state legislature. Today, all states choose their electors by direct statewide election except Maine (1969) and Nebraska (1991), which decided to select two of its electors by a statewide popular vote and the remainder by the popular vote in each congressional district.

ALTHOUGH IT IS generally expected that the electors will cast their vote based on the popular vote within

✪ Electoral votes by state from 1981 through 2010 based on the national census that is undertaken every ten years. The results of the census determine the number of representatives for each state (based on approximately 660,000 people per congressional district). Rising and falling populations change the number of electors within each state, but no state can have fewer than three.

Distribution of Electoral Votes

State	1981–90	1991–2000	2001–10
Alabama	9	9	9
Alaska	3	3	3
Arizona	7	8	10
Arkansas	6	6	6
California	47	54	55
Colorado	8	8	9
Connecticut	8	8	7
Delaware	3	3	3
District of Columbia	3	3	3
Florida	21	25	27
Georgia	12	13	15
Hawaii	4	4	4
Idaho	4	4	4
Illinois	24	22	21
Indiana	12	12	11
Iowa	8	7	7
Kansas	7	6	6
Kentucky	9	8	8
Louisiana	10	9	9
Maine	4	4	4
Maryland	10	10	10

Massachusetts	13	12	12
Michigan	20	18	17
Minnesota	10	10	10
Mississippi	7	7	6
Missouri	11	11	11
Montana	4	3	3
Nebraska	5	5	5
Nevada	4	4	5
New Hampshire	4	4	4
New Jersey	16	15	15
New Mexico	5	5	5
New York	36	33	31
North Carolina	13	14	15
North Dakota	3	3	3
Ohio	23	21	20
Oklahoma	8	8	7
Oregon	7	7	7
Pennsylvania	25	23	21
Rhode Island	4	4	4
South Carolina	8	8	8
South Dakota	3	3	3
Tennessee	11	11	11
Texas	29	32	34
Utah	5	5	5
Vermont	3	3	3
Virginia	12	13	13
Washington	10	11	11
West Virginia	6	5	5
Wisconsin	11	11	10
Wyoming	3	3	3

TOTAL ELECTORAL VOTES: 538
NEEDED TO ELECT A PRESIDENT: 270

their state, there have been 156 "faithless electors" who have, for whatever reason, not voted for their party's designated candidate. None of these electoral votes affected the outcome of an election.

39 Who becomes president of the United States if the president should die?

☞ *The vice president*

40 Who becomes president of the United States if the president and the vice president should die?

☞ *The Speaker of the House of Representatives*

FROM 1792 TO 1886, the president pro tempore of the Senate and the Speaker of the House were next in line after the vice president to succeed the president. This changed in 1886 when the leaders in Congress were replaced in the succession by Cabinet officers, beginning with the secretary of state.

THE PRESIDENTIAL SUCCESSION Act of 1947 established the Speaker of the House as the next in line after the vice president. The president pro tempore of the Senate is next, followed by the members of the Cabinet in the order in which their respective departments were established. The order of succession from within the Cabinet is as follows: secretary of state, secretary of the treasury, secretary of defense, attorney general, secretary of the interior, secretary of agriculture, secretary of commerce, secretary of labor, secretary of health and human services, secretary of housing and urban development, secretary of transportation, secretary of energy, secretary of education, secretary of veterans affairs, and secretary of homeland security.

EIGHT VICE PRESIDENTS succeeded presidents who died while in office: John Tyler (William Henry Harrison died on April 4, 1841, of a cold contracted while giving his inaugural address outside without a hat or scarf); Millard A. Fillmore (Zachary Taylor died of acute indigestion on July 9, 1850); Andrew Johnson (Abraham Lincoln was assassinated by John Wilkes Booth on April 15, 1865); Chester A. Arthur (James Garfield was shot by Charles Guiteau on July 2, 1881, and died on September 19, 1881); Theodore Roosevelt (William McKinley was shot by Leon Czolgosz on September 6, 1901, and died on September 14, 1901); Calvin Coolidge (Warren G. Harding died of a heart attack on August 2, 1923); Harry S. Truman (Franklin D. Roosevelt died on April 12, 1945, of a cerebral hemorrhage); and Lyndon Baines Johnson (John F. Kennedy was assassinated by Lee Harvey Oswald on November 22, 1963).

ACCORDING TO SECTION 2 of the Twenty-fifth Amendment of the Constitution (ratified February 10, 1967): "Whenever there is a vacancy in the office of the Vice President, the President shall nominate a Vice President who shall take office upon confirmation by a majority vote of both Houses of Congress."

THE MORTALITY RATE for sitting vice presidents is almost as high as that for presidents: Seven have died while in office—George Clinton and Elbridge Gerry (both of whom died while serving as James Madison's vice president), William R. D. King (Franklin Pierce), Henry Wilson (Ulysses S. Grant), Thomas A. Hendricks (Grover Cleveland), Garret A. Hobart (William McKinley), and James S. Sherman (William Howard Taft).

VICE PRESIDENT GERALD FORD (who was appointed by Richard M. Nixon after the resignation of Vice President Spiro Agnew) succeeded Nixon, the only president to resign while in office. When Mr. Ford became president, he also became the only person to be appointed—rather than elected—to the two highest offices in the land.

41 What special group advises the president?

☞ *The Cabinet*

THE CONSTITUTION MADE no provision for a president's advisory group. The heads of the three executive departments—state, treasury, and war—and the attorney general, the chief law officer and legal counsel, were organized by George Washington into such a group. The term comes both from the Italian word *gabinetto,* meaning "a small room" (a private meeting place), and from the French *cabinet,* referring in the seventeenth century to a small, private apartment, or "closet," in which the king met privately with his advisers.

THE JUDICIARY ACT of 1789 created the Office of the Attorney General, providing for the appointment of "a meet person, learned in the law, to act as attorney-general for the United States." President Washington needed the attorney general at all the Cabinet meetings to weigh in on the many legal aspects of governing the new nation. The continued presence of the attorney general at Cabinet meetings became the impetus for the position being recognized as a Cabinet post.

CABINET MEMBERS ARE appointed by the president, subject to confirmation by a simple majority of the Senate. Their terms are not fixed, and they may be replaced at any time by the president. At a change in administration, it is customary for Cabinet members to resign, but they remain in office until successors are appointed.

FRANCES PERKINS WAS the first woman appointed to the Cabinet. She served as secretary of labor under Franklin D. Roosevelt beginning in 1933. She lobbied vigorously for passage of the Social Security Act, advocated for higher wages, and worked for legislation to alleviate industrial strife.

PRESIDENT BILL CLINTON appointed Janet Reno as the first female attorney general (1993–2001). He also appointed Madeleine Albright as the first female secretary of state (1997–2001), the highest-ranking Cabinet post.

UNDER PRESIDENT GEORGE W. BUSH, General Colin Powell (2001–2005) became the first African-American to hold the post of secretary of state. He was succeeded by Condoleezza Rice, the first African-American woman to be secretary of state.

42 What is the supreme law of the United States?

....

••

43 What is the Constitution?

••

☞ *The supreme law of the land*

••

(SEE APPENDIX B, page 135, for the complete text of the Constitution and the twenty-seven amendments.)

THE CONSTITUTION IS the cornerstone of the American government. It describes the structure of the government and the rights of its people. No law may be passed that contradicts its principles and no person, or the government, is exempt from following it. This is why it is commonly called the "supreme law of the land."

THE CONSTITUTION BECAME binding by the ratification of the ninth state, New Hampshire, June 21, 1788. On March 3, 1789, the old Confederation went out of existence and on March 4 the new government of the United States began legally to function. On April 6, the organizing of Congress—the legislative branch of the national government—began. On April 30, 1789, George Washington was inaugurated as president of the

United States, making the executive branch of the government operative. On February 2, 1790, the Supreme Court, the head of the third branch of the government—the judicial branch—organized and held its first session, marking the date when our government became fully operative.

> As the British Constitution is the most subtle organism which has proceeded from the womb and long gestation of progressive history, so the American Constitution is, so far as I can see, the most wonderful work ever struck off at a given time by the brain and purpose of man. —William Ewart Gladstone, prime minister of Great Britain (1868–94)

44 In what year was the Constitution written?

···

 1787

···

THE ARTICLES OF Confederation, in place from 1781 to 1789, composed the first official constitution of the United States. The Articles spelled out the organization of the new nation's government as a loose confederation of thirteen independent states, with equal representation in a Congress, to provide for their common defense.

THE FIRST MEETING of the Constitutional Convention, which was convened to revise the Articles of Confederation, took place in Philadelphia in May 1787. Rhode Island was the only state that did not send a delegate. During the course of the convention, it became clear that the Articles could not be revised in a satisfactory manner, and the creation of a new constitution, with a stronger central government, was undertaken.

THE DEPUTIES (DELEGATES) to the Constitutional Convention debated proposed plans until, on July 24, 1787, a substantial agreement was reached. A Committee of Detail was appointed, which delivered a draft on August 6, including a preamble and twenty-three articles, embodying fifty-seven sections. Debate continued until September 8, when a new Committee of Style was named to revise the draft. This committee included William Samuel Johnson of Connecticut, Alexander Hamilton of New York, Gouverneur Morris of Pennsylvania, James Madison of Virginia, and Rufus King of Massachusetts. They submitted the draft in approximately its final shape on September 12. The actual literary form is believed to be largely that of Morris, and the chief evidence for this is in the letters and papers of Madison, and Morris's claim. However, the document was built slowly and laboriously, with every piece shaped and approved. The Preamble was written by the Committee of Style.

ROGER SHERMAN, A delegate from Connecticut, is credited with the creation of the Great Compromise, which established equal representation for each state in the Senate and representation relative to population size in the House of Representatives, thereby responding to the concerns of both the large and small states. He was the only man to sign America's three key documents—the Declaration of Independence, the Articles of Confederation, and the Constitution.

WITHIN THE GREAT COMPROMISE was the Three-fifths Compromise, which provided that, for the purpose of both representation and taxation, a slave would count as three-fifths of a person. This alleviated some of the tension between North and South regarding the balance of power that was rooted in the issue of how to count a slave within the total population. The Three-fifths Compromise was not repealed until 1868 with the ratification of the Fourteenth Amendment.

ON SEPTEMBER 17, 1787, the last day of the Constitutional Convention, eighty-one-year-old Benjamin Franklin (serving as a delegate from Pennsylvania) rose to give a speech to the convention before the signing of the final draft of the Constitution. Too weak to give the speech himself, it was delivered by fellow Pennsylvanian James Wilson.

45 What is the introduction to the Constitution called?

···

☞ *The Preamble*

···

THE PREAMBLE EXPLAINS the purposes of the Constitution and defines the powers of the new government as originating from the people of the United States.

> We the People of the United States, in Order to form a more perfect Union, establish Justice, insure domestic Tranquility, provide for the common defense, promote the general Welfare, and secure the Blessings of Liberty to ourselves and our Posterity, do ordain and establish this Constitution for the United States of America.

46 Can the Constitution be changed?

···

☞ *Yes*

···

47 What do we call a change to the Constitution?

···

☞ *An amendment*

···

THE CONSTITUTION CAN be amended by two methods. By the first method, both the Senate and the House must pass a bill by a two-thirds majority. The bill then goes from Congress to the individual states. Amendments must have the approval of the legislatures or conventions of three-fourths of the existing states before they become part of the Constitution. The second method, which has never been used, requires that a Constitutional Convention be called by at least two-thirds of the legislatures of the states, and calls for that convention to propose one or more amendments. These amendments are then sent to the states to be approved by three-fourths of the legislatures or conventions.

THE PRESIDENT HAS no role in the amendment process. The president cannot veto an amendment proposal or a ratification.

THE FOLLOWING AMENDMENTS were considered by the 108th Congress, which convened in January 2003, but no action was taken on them during the term of that congress.

- To lower the age restriction on senators and representatives from thirty and twenty-five, respectively, to twenty-one
- To ensure that citizens of U.S. territories and commonwealths can vote in presidential elections

- To guarantee the right to use the word *God* in the Pledge of Allegiance and the national motto ("In God we trust")
- To restrict marriage in all states as an institution solely between a man and a woman
- To remove any protection any court may find for child pornography
- To allow Congress to pass laws for emergency replenishment of its membership should more than a quarter of either house be killed
- To place presidential nominees immediately into position, providing the Senate with 120 days to reject the nominee before the appointment is automatically permanent

48 How many changes or amendments are there to the Constitution?

☞ *Twenty-seven*

49 What are the first ten amendments to the Constitution called?

☞ *The Bill of Rights*

50 What is the Bill of Rights?

· ·

☞ *The first ten amendments to the Constitution*

· ·

(SEE APPENDIX B, page 155, for the text of the Bill of Rights.)

THE BILL OF RIGHTS didn't make it into the version of the Constitution that was sent to the states for ratification on September 28, 1787. The lack of such an enumeration of rights, which some feared would open the way to tyranny by the central government, caused two delegates, George Mason and Elbridge Gerry, to refuse to sign the Constitution.

BY SEPTEMBER 1789 there was an increasing sense of urgency regarding the creation and adoption of a Bill of Rights. This was prompted in large part by the demand for such a bill by the states during the ratification process, some of which granted only conditional ratification based on the near-future inclusion of such rights as part of the Constitution. In response the First Congress of the United States proposed twelve amendments, only nine months after the new government under the Constitution formally went into effect on March 4, 1789. The first two proposed amendments, which concerned the number of constituents for each representative and the compensation of members of Congress, were not ratified. The balance, which spell out the immunities of individual citizens, became the first ten amendments to the Constitution, or the Bill of Rights.

51 Name three rights or freedoms guaranteed by the Bill of Rights.

☞ 1. *The right to freedom of speech, press, religion, peaceable assembly, and requesting change of government.*
2. *The right to bear arms (or, the right to have lawful weapons, including firearms, though subject to certain regulations).*
3. *The right to have the government not quarter, or house, soldiers in private homes during peacetime without the owner's consent.*
4. *The guarantee that the government may not search or take a person's property without a warrant.*
5. *The guarantee that a person may not be tried twice by the same jurisdiction for the same crime and cannot be forced to testify against himself or herself.*
6. *The right to a trial and to be represented by a lawyer.*
7. *The right to a jury trial by his/her peers in most cases.*

8. *The right to be protected against excessive or unreasonable fines or cruel and unusual punishment.*
9. *The people have rights other than those mentioned in the Constitution.*
10. *The guarantee that any power not given to the federal government by the Constitution is a power reserved either to the states or to the people.*

....

52 What is the most important right granted to U.S. citizens?

....

 The right to vote

....

53 Name one amendment that guarantees voting rights.

....

 The Fifteenth, Nineteenth, Twenty-fourth, or Twenty-sixth Amendments

....

(SEE APPENDIX B, page 158, for the text of Amendments XI–XXVII to the Constitution.)

Fifteenth Amendment
Passed by Congress February 26, 1869. Ratified February 3, 1870.

Section 1
The right of citizens of the United States to vote shall not be denied or abridged by the United States or by any State on account of race, color, or previous condition of servitude.

Nineteenth Amendment
Passed by Congress June 4, 1919. Ratified August 18, 1920.

The right of citizens of the United States to vote shall not be denied or abridged by the United States or by any State on account of sex.

Twenty-fourth Amendment
Passed by Congress August 27, 1962. Ratified January 23, 1964.

Section 1
The right of citizens of the United States to vote in any primary or other election for President or Vice President, for electors for President or Vice President, or for Senator or Representative in Congress, shall not be denied or abridged by the United States or any State by reason of failure to pay poll tax or other tax.

Twenty-sixth Amendment
Passed by Congress March 23, 1971. Ratified July 1, 1971.

Section 1
The right of citizens of the United States, who are eighteen years of age or older, to vote shall not be denied or

abridged by the United States or by any State on account of age.

54 What is the minimum voting age in the United States?

....

👉 *Eighteen years of age*

....

The Constitution allows states to set qualifications for voting as long as they do not contradict guarantees that are in the Constitution. In order to ensure that any citizen eighteen years or older would be able to vote in all elections, Congress passed the Twenty-sixth Amendment in 1971. Ratified that same year, the Twenty-sixth Amendment was the fastest amendment to be ratified in U.S. history.

Prior to 1971 all but ten states (Alaska, Georgia, Hawaii, Kentucky, Maine, Massachusetts, Minnesota, Montana, Nebraska, and Wyoming) required voters to be at least twenty-one years of age.

55 Name one benefit of being a citizen of the United States.

....

☞ *The ability to vote for the candidate of your choice; travel with a U.S. passport; serve on a jury; apply for federal employment opportunities; and many others.*

....

56 How many branches are there in the government?

....

☞ *Three*

....

57 What are the three branches of our government?

....

☞ *Legislative, executive, and judicial*

....

58 What is the legislative branch of our government?

....

☞ *Congress*

....

59 Who makes the laws in the United States?

....

☞ *Congress*

....

THE FIRST CONGRESS under the current Constitution started its term in Federal Hall in New York City on March 4, 1789, and its first action was to declare that the new Constitution of the United States was in effect. The U.S. Capitol building in Washington, D.C., hosted its first session of Congress on November 17, 1800.

EITHER HOUSE OF Congress has the power to introduce legislation on any subject except for laws dealing with collecting revenue, which must originate in the House of Representatives.

60 What are the duties of Congress?

☞ *To make laws*

61 Who has the power to declare war?

☞ *Congress*

(SEE APPENDIX B, page 141, for the complete text of the Constitution pertaining to the powers of Congress.)

A SELECTION OF congressional powers specified by the Constitution (Article I, Section 8):

- To levy and collect taxes
- To borrow money for the public treasury
- To make rules and regulations governing commerce among the states and with foreign countries
- To make uniform rules for the naturalization of foreign citizens
- To coin money, state its value, and provide for the punishment of counterfeiters
- To set the standards for weights and measures
- To establish bankruptcy laws for the country as a whole
- To establish post offices and post roads
- To issue patents and copyrights
- To set up a system of federal courts
- To punish piracy
- To declare war
- To raise and support armies
- To provide for a navy
- To call out the militia to enforce federal laws, suppress lawlessness, or repel invasions
- To make all laws for the seat of government (Washington, D.C.)

THERE ARE ALSO some acts that Congress cannot undertake, among them:

- Suspending the writ of *habeas corpus*—a requirement that those accused of crimes be brought before a judge or court before being imprisoned—unless necessary in time of rebellion or invasion
- Passing laws that condemn individuals for crimes or unlawful acts without a trial (attainder)
- Passing any law that retroactively makes a specific act a crime

62 What is Congress?

☞ *The Senate and the House of Representatives*

63 Who elects Congress?

☞ *The people*

ORIGINALLY SENATORS WERE selected by their state legislatures. The senatorial selection system became problematic when consecutive legislatures sent different senators to Congress, or when the selection system became corrupted. Some states let the people choose their senators in referenda, which then had to be approved by the legislature. The Seventeenth Amendment to the Constitution, passed by Congress on May 13, 1912, and ratified on April 8, 1913, provided for a uniform method of electing senators directly, in the same manner that representatives were elected.

64 How many senators are there in Congress?

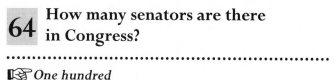

☞ *One hundred*

65 Why are there one hundred senators in the Senate?

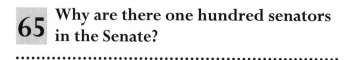

☞ *Two from each state*

66 Can you name the two senators from your state?

☞ *(As of the 2004 election):*

ALABAMA
Richard C. Shelby,
    Republican
Jefferson B. Sessions III,
    Republican

ALASKA
Theodore F. Stevens,
    Republican
Lisa Murkowski, Republican

ARIZONA
John S. McCain III,
    Republican
Jon L. Kyl, Republican

ARKANSAS
Blanche L. Lincoln,
    Democrat
Mark Pryor, Democrat

CALIFORNIA
Dianne G. B. Feinstein,
    Democrat
Barbara L. Boxer, Democrat

COLORADO
Ken Salazar, Democrat
A. Wayne Allard,
    Republican

CONNECTICUT
Christopher J. Dodd,
    Democrat

Joseph I. Lieberman,
    Democrat

DELAWARE
Joseph R. Biden Jr.,
    Democrat
Thomas R. Carper,
    Democrat

FLORIDA
Mel Martinez, Republican
C. William Nelson,
    Democrat

GEORGIA
Johnny Isakson,
    Republican
C. Saxby Chambliss,
    Republican

HAWAII
Daniel K. Inouye, Democrat
Daniel K. Akaka,
    Democrat

IDAHO
Larry E. Craig, Republican
Michael D. Crapo,
    Republican

ILLINOIS
Richard J. Durbin,
    Democrat
Barak Obama, Democrat

INDIANA
Richard G. Lugar,
Republican
B. Evans (Evan) Bayh III,
Democrat

IOWA
Charles E. Grassley,
Republican
Thomas R. Harkin,
Democrat

KANSAS
Samuel D. Brownback,
Republican
C. Patrick Roberts,
Republican

KENTUCKY
A. Mitchell McConnell Jr.,
Republican
James P. D. Bunning,
Republican

LOUISIANA
David Vitter, Republican
Mary L. Landrieu,
Democrat

MAINE
Olympia J. Snowe,
Republican
Susan M. Collins,
Republican

MARYLAND
Paul S. Sarbanes, Democrat
Barbara A. Mikulski,
Democrat

MASSACHUSETTS
Edward M. Kennedy,
Democrat
John F. Kerry, Democrat

MICHIGAN
Carl M. Levin, Democrat
Deborah A. Stabenow,
Democrat

MINNESOTA
Mark Dayton, Democrat
Norm Coleman,
Republican

MISSISSIPPI
W. Thad Cochran,
Republican
C. Trent Lott Jr.,
Republican

MISSOURI
Christopher S. (Kit) Bond,
Republican
James M. Talent,
Republican

MONTANA
Max S. Baucus, Democrat

Conrad R. Burns,
   Republican

Charles T. Hagel,
   Republican
E. Benjamin Nelson,
   Democrat

Harry M. Reid, Democrat
John E. Ensign, Republican

Judd A. Gregg, Republican
John E. Sununu, Republican

Robert Menendez,
   Democrat
Frank R. Lautenberg,
   Democrat

Peter V. Domenici,
   Republican
Jesse F. (Jeff) Bingaman Jr.,
   Democrat

Charles E. Schumer,
   Democrat
Hillary Rodham Clinton,
   Democrat

Richard Burr, Republican
Elizabeth H. Dole,
   Republican

Kent Conrad, Democrat
Byron L. Dorgan,
   Democrat

Michael DeWine,
   Republican
George V. Voinovich,
   Republican

Tom Coburn, Republican
James M. Inhofe, Republican

Ronald L. Wyden,
   Democrat
Gordon H. Smith,
   Republican

Arlen Specter, Republican
Richard J. Santorum,
   Republican

John F. (Jack) Reed,
   Democrat

Lincoln D. Chafee,
    Republican

SOUTH CAROLINA
Jim DeMint, Republican
Lindsey O. Graham,
    Republican

SOUTH DAKOTA
John Thune, Republican
Timothy P. Johnson,
    Democrat

TENNESSEE
William H. Frist,
    Republican
Lamar A. Alexander,
    Republican

TEXAS
Kay Bailey Hutchison,
    Republican
John Cornyn, Republican

UTAH
Orrin G. Hatch, Republican
Robert F. Bennett,
    Republican

VERMONT
Patrick J. Leahy, Democrat

James M. Jeffords,
    Independent

VIRGINIA
John W. Warner,
    Republican
George F. Allen Jr.,
    Republican

WASHINGTON
Patricia Murray, Democrat
Maria E. Cantwell,
    Democrat

WEST VIRGINIA
Robert C. Byrd,
    Democrat
John D. (Jay) Rockefeller IV,
    Democrat

WISCONSIN
Herbert H. Kohl,
    Democrat
Russell D. Feingold,
    Democrat

WYOMING
Craig L. Thomas,
    Republican
Michael B. Enzi,
    Republican

A SENATOR MUST be at least thirty years of age, have been a citizen of the United States for nine years, and, when elected, be a resident of the state from which he or she is chosen.

ON SEPTEMBER 30, 1788, Pennsylvania became the first state to elect its two senators: William Maclay and Robert Morris.

HIRAM R. REVELS (Republican–Mississippi) was the first African-American to be elected; he took his seat in the Senate in 1870.

CHARLES CURTIS (Republican–Kansas) became the first Native American senator to be elected in 1907.

OCTAVIANO LARRAZOLO (Republican–New Mexico) was the first Hispanic senator; he was seated in 1928.

HATTIE OPHELIA WYATT CARAWAY (Democrat–Arkansas) was the first woman elected to the Senate. The governor of Arkansas appointed her to the seat left vacant by the death of her husband, Thaddeus Caraway, assuming that she would hold it only until the next election. Instead, she ran for the office and won an upset victory in 1932. She was subsequently reelected twice, serving until 1945.

CAROL MOSELEY-BRAUN (Democrat–Illinois) became the first African-American woman to take the oath as a senator on January 5, 1993.

FIFTEEN SENATORS HAVE been expelled from the Senate. William Blount, the first senator to be expelled (1797), was charged with treason for aiding the British. The other fourteen were expelled for support of the Confederate States of America.

THE FIRST SPOUSE of a president to be a senator was Democrat Hillary Rodham Clinton, who was elected from New York in 2000.

MANY HAVE SEEN the Senate as a "family business." Huey P. Long (Democrat, 1932–35), his wife, Rose (Democrat, 1935–36), and their son Russell P. Long (Democrat, 1948–87) were senators from Louisiana. The only father and son to serve in the Senate simultaneously were Henry Dodge (Democrat–Wisconsin, 1846–57) and his son, Augustus Dodge (Democrat–Iowa, 1847–54). Millard E. Tydings (Democrat, 1927–50) and his adopted son, Joseph D. Tydings (Democrat, 1965–70) were elected from Maryland. Frank Murkowski (Republican, 1981–2002) and his daughter Lisa Murkowski (Republican, 2001–present) have both represented Alaska. James Asheton Bayard, Sr. (Federalist, 1803–12), and his sons, James

★ James Shields was a traveling man. He is the only person in the history of the Senate to represent three different states: Illinois from 1849 to 1855, Minnesota from 1858 to 1860, and Missouri in 1879.

Asheton Bayard Jr. (Democrat, 1851–64) and Richard Henry Bayard (Democrat, 1851–64, 1867–68), were senators from Delaware. Brothers John F. Kennedy (Democrat, 1953–60) and Edward M. Kennedy (Democrat, 1961–present) have represented Massachusetts, and their brother Robert F. Kennedy (Democrat, 1965–68) represented New York. Elizabeth Dole (Republican, 2003–present), the senator from North Carolina, is the wife of Robert Dole (Republican, 1969–96), who had been the Senate majority leader during part of the time he represented Kansas.

67 For how long do we elect each senator?

....

☞ *A senator's term is six years*

....

There are no limits on the number of terms a senator can serve.

AS OF 2005, Strom Thurmond holds the record for longest service as a senator. Thurmond, a Republican (formerly a Democrat) representing South Carolina, held his seat for forty-seven years and five months. Turning one hundred years old while still in office, he also was the oldest senator ever to serve. He died in December 2003, a year after retiring at the end of his eighth term.

MARGARET CHASE SMITH served longer in the Senate than any other woman. She represented Maine for almost twenty-four years after having served five terms in the House of Representatives. Smith was the first woman to serve in both chambers of Congress.

ROBERT C. BYRD (Democrat–West Virginia) leads all current senators in term of service. He took office in 1959 and began his forty-seventh year in the Senate in January 2006 at age eighty-eight.

REBECCA LATIMER FELTON (Democrat–Georgia), the first female senator, served for just twenty-four hours. Senator Thomas E. Watson died while in office in September 1922. The governor of Georgia, Thomas Hardwick, hoped to win Watson's seat in a special election. He appointed the eighty-seven-year-old Felton to fill the vacancy while Congress was out of session, assuming that she would never serve because she was not a candidate in the upcoming election. Walter F. George beat Hardwick and then allowed Mrs. Felton to present her credentials before he took his seat. Mrs. Felton made a speech to the Senate on November 22, 1922, during her only twenty-four hours as a senator, prior to newly elected Senator George being sworn in.

68 How many representatives are there in Congress?

....

☞ *There are 435 representatives (called congressmen or congresswomen) in the House of Representatives. The number of House members increased as the population expanded through 1913, when 435 became the set number of members. The House also has nonvoting "delegates" from the District of Columbia, American Samoa, Guam, the U.S. Virgin Islands, and a "resident commissioner" from Puerto Rico.*

....

A CONGRESSIONAL DISTRICT comprises about 660,000 people. There are seven states with only one representative: Alaska, Delaware, Montana, North Dakota, South Dakota, Vermont, and Wyoming, giving these states fewer seats in the more populous House than they have in the Senate.

SINCE THE CONGRESS first convened on March 4, 1789, 9,835 members have served in the House of Representatives; of those, 634 members also served in the Senate.

JOSEPH HAYNE RAINEY, a former slave, was the first African-American to serve in the House of Representatives (1870–79), representing South Carolina.

SHIRLEY CHISHOLM (Democrat–New York) was the first African-American woman in Congress. She served in the House of Representatives from 1969–1983 before retiring.

HOUSE DELEGATIONS FOR the first decade of the twenty-first century based on the 2000 census (effective 2001–10):

Alabama (7)
Alaska (1)
Arizona (8)
Arkansas (4)
California (53)
Colorado (7)
Connecticut (5)
Delaware (1)
Florida (25)
Georgia (13)
Hawaii (2)
Idaho (2)
Illinois (19)
Indiana (9)
Iowa (5)
Kansas (4)
Kentucky (6)
Louisiana (7)

Maine (2)
Maryland (8)
Massachusetts (10)
Michigan (15)
Minnesota (8)
Mississippi (4)
Missouri (9)
Montana (1)
Nebraska (3)
Nevada (3)
New Hampshire (2)
New Jersey (13)
New Mexico (3)
New York (29)
North Carolina (13)

North Dakota (1)
Ohio (18)
Oklahoma (5)
Oregon (5)
Pennsylvania (19)
Rhode Island (2)
South Carolina (6)
South Dakota (1)
Tennessee (9)
Texas (32)
Utah (3)
Vermont (1)
Virginia (11)
Washington (9)
West Virginia (3)
Wisconsin (8)
Wyoming (1)

69 For how long do we elect representatives?

....

☞ *A representative's term is two years*

....

THERE ARE NO limits on the number of terms a representative can serve. Since the entire House of Representatives is elected every two years, a "new" Congress convenes every two years, in the January following a November election. The first Congress convened in 1789. The 108th Congress, elected on November 2, 2002, took office in January 2003.

AFTER SERVING ONE term as president (1825–29), John Quincy Adams was elected to Congress from his home district in Massachusetts. He served nine consecutive terms in the House of Representatives (first as a Whig and later as a Republican), earning the nickname "Old Man Eloquent" because of his extraordinary speeches in opposition to slavery. Adams won more acclaim for his long congressional career than for his earlier presidency. He suffered a stroke on the floor of the House on February 21, 1848, and died two days later.

THOMAS BRACKETT REED (Republican–Maine) served in Congress from 1877 to 1899 (twelve terms) during which time he served twice as Speaker of the House (1889–91; 1895–99). As Speaker his procedural changes strengthened legislative control by the majority party and increased the power of the Speaker and the Rules Committee. His opponents dubbed him "Czar Reed" for his vigorous promotion of the passage of those changes, known as "Reed's Rules."

70 Who signs bills into laws?

....

☞ *The president*

....

ACCORDING TO *Our American Government* (2000 Edition, printed by the authority of the 106th Congress): "The President has three choices: First, to sign a bill within 10 days (Sundays excepted), whereupon it becomes a law. Second, the President may veto the bill, i.e., return it to Congress (stating objections) without a signature of approval. In this case, Congress may override the veto with a two-thirds vote in each House. The bill would then become a law despite the President's veto. The House and Senate are not required to attempt veto overrides. Third, the President may hold the bill without taking any action. Two different developments may occur in this situation depending upon whether Congress is in session. If Congress is in session, the bill becomes law after the expiration of 10 days (excluding Sundays), even without the President's signature. If Congress has adjourned, the bill does not become law; this is called a 'pocket veto.'"

71 What is the judicial branch of our government?

☞ *The Supreme Court*

72 What is the highest court in the United States?

☞ *The Supreme Court*

73 What are the duties of the Supreme Court?

☞ *To interpret the constitutionality of laws*

THE AUTHORITY OF the Supreme Court as the highest in the land originates from Article III of the Constitution. The Supreme Court is the ultimate arbiter of all cases and controversies in which there is a need to interpret the Constitution. When the Court agrees to hear a case, its sole intention is to examine and clarify a point of law, not to adjudicate individual or collective guilt or innocence in a criminal case. The Court decides if a law or government action violates the Constitution. Judicial review enables the Court to invalidate both federal and state laws when they conflict with the Constitution. The decisions of the Court can be changed only by another Supreme Court decision or by a Constitutional amendment.

74 Who selects the Supreme Court justices?

....

☞ *The president appoints them*

....

THE CONSTITUTION GIVES the president the power to nominate Supreme Court justices, but all Supreme Court nominations must be confirmed by a majority vote in the Senate.

AS OF 2004, 148 people had been officially nominated to the Supreme Court. The Senate has rejected 12, taken no action on 5, and postponed votes on 3. The president has withdrawn a nominee six times. Seven others have declined the nomination.

THE FRAMERS OF the Constitution wanted to ensure that members of the Supreme Court would be free from political pressure, so the Constitution provides that, once appointed, justices may remain in office "during good behavior" until they die or choose to retire. Their independence is further protected by a constitutional guarantee that their salaries will not be diminished while they are in office. In 2004, the chief justice of the Supreme Court was paid $202,900 a year, while an associate justice was paid $194,200 per year.

GEORGE WASHINGTON SET a high standard when he nominated justices "with a sole view to the public good" and to "bring forward those who, upon every consideration and from the best information I can obtain, will in my judgment be most likely to answer that great end." Washington named only men he knew well; and he measured them against specific criteria, including the fitness of their character and health, rigorous training, and public recognition.

75 How many Supreme Court justices are there?

••

☞ *There are nine justices: A chief and eight associates*

••

THE CURRENT COURT consists of Chief Justice John G. Roberts Jr. (2005), John Paul Stevens (1975), Antonin Scalia (1986), Anthony M. Kennedy (1988), David Hackett Souter (1990), Clarence Thomas

(1991), Ruth Bader Ginsburg (1993), Stephen G. Breyer (1994), and Samuel Anthony Alito Jr. (2006).

THE FIRST SUPREME Court had six members and there have been as many as ten seats on the bench. Although it falls to Congress to legislate the number of judges on the High Court, President Franklin D. Roosevelt, in an effort to bolster his New Deal programs, supported "Court-packing" legislation to increase the number of justices on the Court.

IT'S EASY TO see who has been on the Supreme Court the longest. In the Court the justices are seated by seniority, with the chief justice in the center, the senior associate justice to the chief's right, the second senior to the chief's left, and so on, alternating right and left.

THE TRADITION OF the "conference handshake" began with Chief Justice Melville W. Fuller (1888–1910). Before they take their seats at the bench, each justice shakes hands with the others. Fuller cited the practice as a way to remind the justices that, although they may have differences of opinion, they share a common purpose.

LEVI WOODBURY (1845–51), nominated by James K. Polk, was the first Supreme Court justice to actually attend a law school.

★ Although he was a deliberate jurist, Justice Byron R. White (1962–93) was a swift runner. "Whizzer" White led the National Football League in rushing in 1938 as a running back for the Pittsburgh Pirates (now the Steelers).

THURGOOD MARSHALL (1967–91), nominated by Lyndon Baines Johnson, was the first African-American to become an associate justice. Prior to sitting on its bench, he represented and won more cases before the Supreme Court than any other American.

SANDRA DAY O'CONNOR (1981–present), nominated by Ronald Reagan, was the first woman to serve as a justice of the Supreme Court.

76 Who is the chief justice of the United States?

☞ *John G. Roberts, Jr.*

JOHN G. ROBERTS, JR. is the fifteenth chief justice of the United States. Nominated by President George W. Bush to take the seat of retiring Justice Sandra Day O'Connor, his nomination was quickly changed to fill the position of chief justice when the incumbent, William H. Rehnquist, died in September 2005.

THE CHIEF JUSTICE of the United States is the head of the judicial branch of the government of the United States, and presides over the Supreme Court. The chief justice also officiates at the inauguration of the president of the United States and presides when the Senate tries impeachments of the president.

CHIEF JUSTICE JOHN MARSHALL (1801–35) authored an opinion in the landmark case of *Marbury v. Madison* (1803), which is considered, two hundred years later, the cornerstone of the principle of judicial review. It gives the Court the authority to invalidate any law that it finds to be unconstitutional. Chief Justice Marshall also understood the value of job security; he held his seat for more than thirty-four years and was the first chief justice to die while on the bench. Oliver Ellsworth, however, had other things on his mind; he resigned in 1801 after sitting for four years, nine months, the shortest stay.

CHIEF JUSTICE ROGER B. TANEY (1836–64) has the ignominious distinction of having delivered the majority opinion in the *Dred Scott* case (*Dred Scott v. Sandford*, 1857), which held that a person who was a slave in Missouri but had traveled to a free state to obtain his freedom was still a slave. The Court's opinion read, in part, "We think they [people of African ancestry] are not included, and were not intended to be included, under the word citizens in the Constitution, and can therefore claim none of the rights and privileges which that instrument provides for and secures to citizens of the United States."

EDWARD D. WHITE (associate justice, 1894–1910; chief justice, 1910–21) understood shades of gray. He was a veteran of the Civil War, having fought on the Confederate side. White also holds the distinction of having been the only person promoted to chief justice by the man who would succeed him, President William Howard Taft. Taft, in turn, is the only person to have been both president of the United States and chief justice of the United States.

WARREN BURGER, WHO was named chief justice by President Richard Nixon, spoke for a unanimous Court (*United States v. Nixon,* 1974) upholding a subpoena for the Watergate tapes, which led to that president's resignation.

★ Melville W. Fuller was chief justice (1888–1910) during the only criminal trial presided over by the Supreme Court. In November 1909 Sheriff Joseph F. Shipp, his deputy sheriff, and four members of a Chattanooga, Tennessee, mob were convicted on criminal contempt charges after Ed Johnson, a black carpenter, was lynched. Mr. Johnson was taken from an "undermanned jail" in Sheriff Shipp's jurisdiction, after a stay of his execution was ordered by the Supreme Court.

77 What is the capital of your state?

••

☞ *State Capitals:*

••

ALABAMA: Montgomery (1847)

ALASKA: Juneau (1959; territorial capital 1912)

ARKANSAS: Little Rock (1836)

ARIZONA: Phoenix (1912; territorial capital 1889)

CALIFORNIA: Sacramento (1854)

COLORADO: Denver (1867)

CONNECTICUT: Hartford (1874; cocapital with New Haven 1635)

DELAWARE: Dover (1777)

FLORIDA: Tallahassee (1845)

GEORGIA: Atlanta (1887)

HAWAII: Honolulu (1959; kingdom capital 1850)

IDAHO: Boise (1890; territorial capital 1864)

ILLINOIS: Springfield (1837)

INDIANA: Indianapolis (1825)

IOWA: Des Moines (1857)

KANSAS: Topeka (1861)

KENTUCKY: Frankfort (1792).

LOUISIANA: Baton Rouge (1882)

MAINE: Augusta (1831)

MARYLAND: Annapolis (1788; colonial capital 1694)

MASSACHUSETTS: Boston (1788; colonial capital 1632)

MICHIGAN: Lansing (1847)

MINNESOTA: St. Paul (1858; territorial capital 1849)

MISSISSIPPI: Jackson (1821)

MISSOURI: Jefferson City (1826)

MONTANA: Helena (1889; territorial capital 1875)

NEBRASKA: Lincoln (1867)

NEVADA: Carson City (1864)

NEW HAMPSHIRE: Concord (1808)

NEW JERSEY: Trenton (1790)

NEW MEXICO: Santa Fe (1912; territorial capital 1861)

NEW YORK: Albany (1797)

NORTH CAROLINA: Raleigh (1792)

NORTH DAKOTA: Bismarck (1889)

OHIO: Columbus (1816)

OREGON: Salem (1864)

OKLAHOMA: Oklahoma City (1910)

PENNSYLVANIA: Harrisburg (1812)

RHODE ISLAND: Providence (1900; cocapital with Newport 1790)

SOUTH CAROLINA: Columbia (1786)

SOUTH DAKOTA: Pierre (1890)

TENNESSEE: Nashville (1843)

TEXAS: Austin (1845)

UTAH: Salt Lake City (1896; territorial capital 1850)

VERMONT: Montpelier (1805)

VIRGINIA: Richmond (1779)

WASHINGTON: Olympia (1889; territorial capital 1853)

WEST VIRGINIA: Charleston (1885)

WISCONSIN: Madison (1848; territorial capital 1836)

WYOMING: Cheyenne (1869)

78 What is the chief executive of a state government called?

••

☞ *The governor*

••

79 Who is the current governor of your state?

☞ *(As of the 2004 election):*

ALABAMA
Bob Riley, Republican

ALASKA
Frank Murkowski,
    Republican

ARIZONA
Janet Napolitano, Democrat

ARKANSAS
Mike Huckabee, Republican

CALIFORNIA
Arnold Schwarzenegger,
    Republican

COLORADO
Bill Owens, Republican

CONNECTICUT
M. Jodi Rell, Republican

DELAWARE
Ruth Ann Minner,
    Democrat

FLORIDA
Jeb Bush, Republican

GEORGIA
Sonny Perdue, Republican

HAWAII
Linda Lingle, Republican

IDAHO
Dirk Kempthorne,
    Republican

ILLINOIS
Rod Blagojevich, Democrat

INDIANA
Mitchell E. Daniels,
    Republican

IOWA
Thomas Vilsack, Democrat

KANSAS
Kathleen Sebelius,
    Democrat

KENTUCKY
Ernie Fletcher, Republican

LOUISIANA
Kathleen Blanco, Democrat

MAINE
John Baldacci, Democrat

MARYLAND
Robert Ehrlich,
    Republican

MASSACHUSETTS
Mitt Romney, Republican

MICHIGAN
Jennifer Granholm,
    Democrat

MINNESOTA
Tim Pawlenty, Republican

MISSISSIPPI
Haley Barbour, Republican

MISSOURI
Matt Blunt, Republican

MONTANA
Brian Schweitzer,
    Republican

NEBRASKA
Dave Heineman, Republican

NEVADA
Kenny Guinn, Republican

NEW HAMPSHIRE
John Lynch, Democrat

NEW JERSEY
Jon S. Corzine, Democrat

NEW MEXICO
Bill Richardson, Democrat

NEW YORK
George Pataki, Republican

NORTH CAROLINA
Michael Easley, Democrat

NORTH DAKOTA
John Hoeven, Republican

OHIO
Bob Taft, Republican

OKLAHOMA
Brad Henry, Democrat

OREGON
Ted Kulongoski, Democrat

PENNSYLVANIA
Edward Rendell, Democrat

RHODE ISLAND
Don Carcieri, Republican

SOUTH CAROLINA
Mark Sanford, Republican

SOUTH DAKOTA
Mike Rounds, Republican

TENNESSEE
Phil Bredesen, Democrat

TEXAS
Rick Perry, Republican

UTAH
Jon Huntsman, Republican

VERMONT
James H. Douglas,
    Republican

VIRGINIA
Tim Kaine, Democrat

WASHINGTON
Christine Gregoire,
    Democrat

WEST VIRGINIA
Joe Manchin III, Democrat

WISCONSIN
Jim Doyle, Democrat

WYOMING
Dave Freudenthal,
    Democrat

⭐ These seventeen state governors were elected president: Thomas Jefferson (Virginia), James Monroe (Virginia), Martin Van Buren (New York), John Tyler (Virginia), James Polk (Tennessee), Andrew Johnson (Tennessee) , Rutherford B. Hayes (Ohio), Grover Cleveland (New York), William McKinley (Ohio), Theodore Roosevelt (New York), Woodrow Wilson (New Jersey), Calvin Coolidge (Massachusetts), Franklin D. Roosevelt (New York), Jimmy Carter (Georgia), Ronald Reagan (California), Bill Clinton (Arkansas), George W. Bush (Texas).

80 What is the chief executive of a city government called?

☞ *The mayor*

••

MORE THAN 50,000 cities and towns in the United States have mayors.

81 Who was president during the Civil War?

••

☞ *Abraham Lincoln*

••

LINCOLN THOUGHT SECESSION was illegal, and was willing to use force to defend federal law and the Union. When Confederate batteries fired on Fort Sumter in 1861 and forced its surrender, he called on the states for seventy-five thousand volunteers. Four more slave states joined the Confederacy but four remained within the Union. The Civil War had begun, and it lasted until 1865. More than 620,000 soldiers on both sides died during the war.

82 What did the Emancipation Proclamation do?

••

☞ *Freed many slaves*

••

83 Which president freed the slaves?

☞ *Abraham Lincoln*

(SEE APPENDIX C, page 173, for the full text of the Emancipation Proclamation.)

ON SEPTEMBER 22, 1862, after the Union Army victory at Antietam, Maryland, President Lincoln issued a preliminary proclamation, stating that on January 1, 1863, he would free all the slaves in those states still in rebellion. The decree left room for a plan of compensated emancipation.

PRESIDENT LINCOLN SIGNED the final draft of the Emancipation Proclamation on January 1, 1863. It applied only to states that had seceded from the Union, effectively leaving slavery intact in the loyal border states. "All persons held as slaves within any State or designated part of the State, the people whereof shall then be in rebellion against the United States, shall be then, thenceforward, and forever free." Since the states that this affected no longer considered themselves to be under the jurisdiction of President Lincoln, the freedom he promised ultimately depended on a military victory by the Union. This irony was not lost on Secretary of State William Seward, who said, "We show our sympathy with slavery by emancipating slaves where we cannot reach them and holding them in bondage where we can set them free."

THE EMANCIPATION PROCLAMATION signaled the acceptance of black men into the Union Army and Navy. By the end of the Civil War almost two hundred thousand black soldiers and sailors had fought for the Union.

THE OFFICIAL END of slavery in America was achieved by the ratification of the Thirteenth Amendment to the Constitution on December 18, 1865, which read in part (Section 1): "Neither slavery nor involuntary servitude, except as a punishment for crime whereof the party shall have been duly convicted, shall exist within the United States, or any place subject to their jurisdiction."

⭐ A manuscript of the final version of the Emancipation Proclamation in Lincoln's hand, owned by the Chicago Historical Society, was destroyed in that city's famous fire in 1871. A manuscript version of the Preliminary Emancipation Proclamation, owned by New York State, was saved from the same fate in a fire in Albany, New York, in 1911.

84 What is the name of the president's official home?

☞ *The White House*

85 What is the White House?

☞ *The official residence of the president*

PRESIDENT WASHINGTON AND city planner Pierre L'Enfant chose the site for the new residence. Architect James Hoban won a gold medal from the U.S. government for his design of the President's House, for which the Masonic cornerstone ceremony was held on October 13, 1792.

⭐ The laying of Masonic cornerstones has preceded the construction of many important structures in the United States, including the Capitol building, the Washington Monument, the Erie Canal, the Battle of Bunker Hill Monument, the Statue of Liberty, and the National Cathedral. A number of Founding Fathers, including Benjamin Franklin, John Hancock, Paul Revere, and George Washington were members of the fraternal order known as the Freemasons.

THE FIRST OFFICIAL name of the White House was the President's House and later, the Executive Mansion. It first took on its now familiar color in 1798 because of the limestone whitewash that was applied to protect the stone from freezing as it was being built. It has been popularly referred to as the White House since the early 1800s, but President Theodore Roosevelt made the *White House* the official name of the residence in September 1901.

THE WHITE HOUSE survived a fire at the hands of the British in 1814 (during the War of 1812) and a fire in the West Wing in 1929, while Herbert Hoover was president.

THE WHITE HOUSE contains the living quarters for the president and the president's family, while providing offices for the president and the president's staff. There are 132 rooms in the fifty-five thousand-square-foot structure located on eighteen acres of land.

GEORGE WASHINGTON IS the only president who never lived in Washington, D.C., although a 1797 portrait of Washington, obtained in 1800, is the oldest remaining possession in the White House. John and Abigail Adams were the first to occupy the residence, while it was still under construction in 1800.

THE WEST WING was built in 1902 during the administration of Theodore Roosevelt. However, the Oval Office, which we now think of as synonymous with the president, was built for William Howard Taft, who first used it in 1909, almost 110 years after John Adams first moved in.

THERE HAVE BEEN seventeen nuptials performed at the White House. The first one, in 1812, was that of Lucy Payne Washington (sister to Dolley Madison) to Supreme Court Justice Thomas Todd. Grover Cleveland was the only president to be married there while in office, when he wed Frances Folsom in 1886.

IN 1974 CONGRESS turned the house at the Naval Observatory into the official residence of the vice president. Although it was available to the Fords and the Rockefellers, neither family lived there. Walter Mondale was the first vice president to move into the home.

⭐ Care to visit the White House? For the most up-to-date information about touring and visiting, call the twenty-four-hour Visitors Office Information Line at (202) 456–7041.

86 Where is the White House located?

☞ At 1600 Pennsylvania Avenue NW, Washington, D.C. (the District of Columbia)

IN DECEMBER OF 1790, George Washington signed the Residency Act that declared that the federal government would reside in a district "not exceeding 10 miles square . . . on the river Potomac." Washington, D.C., is not part of any state. It is a unique, federally managed district within the United States, which is allowed to exercise limited local rule.

ON DECEMBER 1, 1800, the federal capital was transferred from Philadelphia to the site on the Potomac River now called the city of Washington, in the territory of Columbia (so named in honor of Christopher Columbus).

THE LAND THAT became the District of Columbia was ceded by two slave states, Maryland and Virginia. Sadly, the majority of the labor force used to build the White House and the U.S. Capitol were African-American slaves.

CONGRESS ABOLISHED SLAVERY in the federal district on April 16, 1862, predating the Emancipation Proclamation and the adoption of the Thirteenth Amendment to the Constitution.

THE RESIDENTS OF the nation's capital were given the right to vote in a presidential election in 1961 when the Twenty-third Amendment to the Constitution was ratified.

IN 1970 LEGISLATION authorized election of a nonvoting delegate from the District of Columbia to the House of Representatives. In 1993 this delegate gained the right to vote on the floor of the House in cases where the delegate's votes would be deemed not to be decisive. Even this limited right to vote was overturned by Congress in 1995.

THE 1978 D.C. Voting Rights Amendment provided for federal voting rights (the same as those for residents of the fifty states) for residents of D.C. Although the amendment was passed in both Houses of Congress, it did not receive ratification by three-quarters of the states prior to a seven-year deadline.

87 Who was Martin Luther King Jr.?

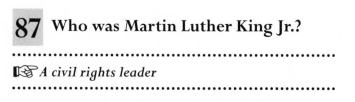

☞ *A civil rights leader*

MARTIN LUTHER KING JR. was born Michael but later had his name changed by his father in honor of the Protestant reformer Martin Luther.

THE REVEREND DR. KING was the president of the Montgomery (Alabama) Improvement Association, the organization that was responsible for the successful Montgomery Bus Boycott from 1955 to 1956 (381 days). On December 21, 1956, after the Supreme Court had declared unconstitutional the laws requiring segregation on buses, blacks and whites rode the buses as equals.

BETWEEN 1957 AND 1968 Dr. King traveled more than six million miles and spoke some twenty-five hundred times, preaching nonviolent resistance in an effort to achieve civil rights and racial equality for African-Americans and other people of color.

DR. KING WAS one of the leaders of The March on Washington for Jobs and Freedom on August 28, 1963, which was attended by approximately 250,000 people, making it the largest demonstration seen in the nation's capital to that date. The "I Have a Dream" speech he delivered that day was a cornerstone of the civil rights movement.

DR. KING WAS named Man of the Year by *Time* magazine in 1963.

IN 1964, AT age thirty-five, Dr. King became the youngest man to receive the Nobel Peace Prize. He was the second American to be awarded the prestigious prize (the first having been Dr. Ralph J. Bunche, who received the prize in 1950 for his work as a United Nations mediator leading to the 1949 Arab-Israeli armistice agreement), and the third black man (the second having been Albert John Luthuli [1960] of Rhodesia, who led a nonviolent struggle against inequality in his homeland).

DR. KING'S ABILITY to focus attention and mobilize public opinion was an important contributing factor in the passage by Congress of the Civil Rights Act of 1964, outlawing segregation in public accommodations and discrimination in education and employment, and the Voting Rights Act of 1965, which suspended (later banned) literacy tests and other restrictions to prevent blacks from voting.

DR. KING WAS assassinated on April 4, 1968, in Memphis, Tennessee, by James Earl Ray.

88 Which countries were our principal allies during World War II?

☞ *Australia, Canada, China, France, New Zealand, the Soviet Union, and the United Kingdom*

89 Which countries were our enemies during World War II?

☞ *Germany, Italy, and Japan*

An abridged time line of World War II from 1939 through 1945:

March 15, 1939	The German Army invades Czechoslovakia
March 23, 1939	Adolf Hitler threatens to seize the city of Danzig, Poland
March 29, 1939	Britain and France pledge to support Poland
April 7, 1939	Italy invades Albania
August 23, 1939	Joseph Stalin and Adolf Hitler sign the Nazi-Soviet Pact.
September 1, 1939	The German Army invades Poland and annexes the free city of Danzig
September 3, 1939	Britain and France declare war on Nazi Germany
September 17, 1939	The Soviet Union's Red Army invades Poland
September 21, 1939	The Germans announce that all Jews in Poland are to be imprisoned in ghettos
September 27, 1939	The Polish Army surrenders in Warsaw

October 3, 1939	Franklin D. Roosevelt announces that the United States will remain neutral in the European war
November 1, 1939	Germany annexes western Poland
November 2, 1939	The Soviet Union annexes eastern Poland
November 20, 1939	The Red Army invades Finland
December 14, 1939	The Soviet Union is expelled from the League of Nations
March 28, 1940	Britain and France agree not to sign a separate peace with Nazi Germany
April 9, 1940	The German Army invades Denmark and Norway
June 4, 1940	The last of the 338,000 British, French, and Belgian forces are evacuated from Dunkirk
June 10, 1940	Italy's Benito Mussolini declares war on the Allies
June 14, 1940	The German Army enters Paris
June 15, 1940	The United States rejects France's renewed appeal for assistance against the German Army
June 22, 1940	France signs an armistice with Germany
July 10, 1940	The Luftwaffe launches the start of the Battle of Britain
August 23, 1940	The Luftwaffe carries out an all-night bombing raid on London and begins the Blitz

August 25, 1940	The Royal Air Force bombs Berlin
September 27, 1940	Yosuke Matsuoka of Japan signs the Tripartite Pact with Nazi Germany and Italy
October 28, 1940	The Italian Army invades Greece
March 1, 1941	Bulgaria signs the Tripartite Pact and joins forces with Germany, Italy, and Japan
March 7, 1941	The British Army invades Italian-controlled Ethiopia
March 11, 1941	The U.S. Congress passes the Lend-Lease Act
April 6, 1941	The Italian Army in Ethiopia surrenders to Allied forces
April 10, 1941	Germany, Italy, and Bulgaria invade Yugoslavia
April 14, 1941	Japan signs a nonaggression pact with the Soviet Union
April 17, 1941	Yugoslavia surrenders to the German Army
April 21, 1941	Greece surrenders to the German Army
July 12, 1941	The Soviet Union and Britain sign an agreement of mutual aid
August 12, 1941	The German Army advances on Leningrad
September 20, 1941	The German Army captures Kiev, the Ukrainian capital in the Soviet Union

October 6, 1941	The German Army advances on Moscow
December 1, 1941	Emperor Hirohito officially approves the attack on the United States
December 7, 1941	Japanese forces attack the American fleet at Pearl Harbor
December 22, 1941	The Japanese Army captures Manila, the capital of the Philippines
January 29, 1942	The U.S. government announces the establishment of relocation camps for Japanese Americans
February 22, 1942	General Douglas MacArthur and the U.S. forces leave the Philippines
April 18, 1942	The U.S. Air Force bombs Tokyo
June 3, 1942	Start of the Battle of Midway
August 24, 1942	The German Army enters Stalingrad
November 4, 1942	The German Army is defeated at El Alamein in the deserts of North Africa
November 11, 1942	Adolf Hitler orders the occupation of Vichy France
January 23, 1943	The Allies capture Tripoli
February 25, 1943	British and American military aircraft begin round-the-clock bombing of Nazi Germany
May 7, 1943	The Allies capture Tunis

July 10, 1943	Allied troops land on German-occupied Sicily
September 23, 1943	Italy's new prime minister, Pietro Badoglio, signs an armistice with the Allies
October 13, 1943	Italy declares war on Germany
December 28, 1943	Winston Churchill, Franklin D. Roosevelt, and Joseph Stalin meet at Tehran in Iran
January 22, 1944	The U.S. Fifth Army lands at Anzio, Italy
May 18, 1944	Allied troops take Monte Cassino, Italy
June 6, 1944	D-Day: Allies land at Normandy, France
August 24, 1944	The U.S. Army enters Paris
September 11, 1944	Allied troops enter Nazi Germany
September 11, 1944	Winston Churchill and Franklin D. Roosevelt meet in Quebec to discuss postwar Germany
October 2, 1944	Nazi Germany crushes the Warsaw Uprising
October 9, 1944	Winston Churchill, Joseph Stalin, and Franklin D. Roosevelt meet in Moscow
October 20, 1944	General Douglas MacArthur returns to the Philippines
January 17, 1945	The Red Army liberates Warsaw
February 4, 1945	Winston Churchill, Joseph Stalin, and Franklin D. Roosevelt meet at the Yalta Conference in the Crimea

February 19, 1945	The U.S. Army lands on Iwo Jima, Japan
February 28, 1945	The U.S. Army captures Manila, the capital of the Philippines
May 8, 1945	Winston Churchill announces VE (Victory in Europe) day
July 16, 1945	Manhattan Project scientists test the atom bomb at Alamogordo, New Mexico
August 6, 1945	U.S. Army Air Force drops an atom bomb on Hiroshima, Japan
August 9, 1945	U.S. Army Air Force drops an atom bomb on Nagasaki, Japan
September 2, 1945	General Douglas MacArthur accepts the Japanese surrender in Tokyo Bay

90 Name one purpose of the United Nations.

☞ *To discuss and try to resolve world problems*

THE NAME *UNITED NATIONS* was coined by President Franklin D. Roosevelt in the "Declaration by United Nations" of January 1, 1942, during World War II, when representatives of twenty-six nations pledged their governments to continue fighting together against the Axis powers of Germany, Japan, and Italy.

THE UNITED NATIONS officially came into existence on October 24, 1945, when the UN Charter was ratified by a majority of the original fifty-one member states, including the United States. It succeeded the defunct League of Nations as a world body. The League was created in 1919 in the aftermath of World War I, but disintegrated during the 1930s. President Woodrow Wilson was a primary architect of the League of Nations but, ironically, the Senate's failure to ratify its charter precluded the United States from becoming a member state.

THE LAND FOR UN headquarters in New York City was donated by John D. Rockefeller Jr. and is considered international territory, which means diplomatic laws rather than local municipal laws are applied to foreign nationals who work there.

FOLLOWING IS AN alphabetical list of the 191 member states of the United Nations with the date on which each one joined the organization.

Member and Date of Admission:
Afghanistan 11/19/46, Albania 12/14/55, Algeria 10/8/62, Andorra 7/28/93, Angola 12/1/76, Antigua and Barbuda 11/11/81, Argentina 10/24/45, Armenia 3/2/92, Australia 11/1/45, Austria 12/14/55, Azerbaijan 3/2/92, Bahamas 9/18/73, Bahrain 9/21/71, Bangladesh 9/17/74, Barbados 12/9/66, Belarus (formerly Byelorussia) 10/24/45, Belgium

12/27/45, Belize 9/25/81, Benin 9/20/60, Bhutan
9/21/71, Bolivia 11/14/45, Bosnia and Herzegovina
5/22/92, Botswana 10/17/66, Brazil 10/24/45, Brunei
Darussalam 9/21/84, Bulgaria 12/14/55, Burkina Faso
9/20/60, Burundi 9/18/62, Cambodia 12/14/55, Cameroon
9/20/60, Canada 11/9/45, Cape Verde 9/16/75, Central
African Republic 9/20/60, Chad 9/20/60, Chile 10/24/45,
China 10/24/45, Colombia 11/5/45, Comoros 11/12/75,
Congo 9/20/60, Costa Rica 11/2/45, Côte d'Ivoire 9/20/60,
Croatia 5/22/92, Cuba 10/24/45, Cyprus 9/20/60, Czech
Republic 1/19/93, Democratic People's Republic of Korea
(North Korea) 9/17/91, Democratic Republic of the Congo
9/20/60, Denmark 10/24/45, Djibouti 9/20/77, Dominica
12/18/78, Dominican Republic 10/24/45, Ecuador 12/21/45,
Egypt 10/24/45, El Salvador 10/24/45, Equatorial Guinea
11/12/68, Eritrea 5/28/93, Estonia 9/17/91, Ethiopia
11/13/45, Fiji 10/13/70, Finland 12/14/55, France
10/24/45, Gabon 9/20/60, Gambia 9/21/65, Georgia
7/31/92, Germany—(comprising the former Federal
Republic of Germany and the former German Democratic
Republic) 9/18/73, Ghana 3/8/57, Greece 10/25/45,
Grenada 9/17/74, Guatemala 11/21/45, Guinea 12/12/58,
Guinea-Bissau 9/17/74, Guyana 9/20/66, Haiti 10/24/45,
Honduras 12/17/45, Hungary 12/14/55, Iceland 11/19/46,
India 10/30/45, Indonesia 9/28/50, Iran (Islamic Republic of)
10/24/45, Iraq 12/21/45, Ireland 12/14/55, Israel 5/11/49,
Italy 12/14/55, Jamaica 9/18/62, Japan 12/18/56, Jordan
12/14/55, Kazakhstan 3/2/92, Kenya 12/16/63, Kiribati
9/14/99, Kuwait 5/14/63, Kyrgyzstan 3/2/92, Lao People's
Democratic Republic 12/14/55, Latvia 9/17/91, Lebanon
10/24/45, Lesotho 10/17/66, Liberia 11/2/45, Libyan Arab
Jamahiriya 12/14/55, Liechtenstein 9/18/90, Lithuania
9/17/91, Luxembourg 10/24/45, Macedonia (former

Yugoslav Republic of) 4/8/93, Madagascar 9/20/60, Malawi 12/1/64, Malaysia 9/17/57, Maldives 9/21/65, Mali 9/28/60, Malta 12/1/64, Marshall Islands 9/17/91, Mauritania 10/27/61, Mauritius 4/24/68, Mexico 11/7/45, Micronesia (Federated States of) 9/17/91, Monaco 5/28/93, Mongolia 10/27/61, Morocco 11/12/56, Mozambique 9/16/75, Myanmar 4/19/48, Namibia 4/23/90, Nauru 9/14/99, Nepal 12/14/55, Netherlands 12/10/45, New Zealand 10/24/45, Nicaragua 10/24/45, Niger 9/20/60, Nigeria 10/7/60, Norway 11/27/45, Oman 10/7/71, Pakistan 9/30/47, Palau 12/15/94, Panama 11/13/45, Papua New Guinea 10/10/75, Paraguay 10/24/45, Peru 10/31/45, Philippines 10/24/45, Poland 10/24/45, Portugal 12/14/55, Qatar 9/21/71, Republic of Korea (South Korea) 9/17/91, Republic of Moldova 3/2/92, Romania 12/14/55, Russian Federation (formerly the USSR) 10/24/55, Rwanda 9/18/62, St. Kitts and Nevis 9/23/83, St. Lucia 9/18/79, St. Vincent and the Grenadines 9/16/80, Samoa 12/15/76, San Marino 3/2/92, São Tomé and Princípe 9/16/75, Saudi Arabia 10/24/45, Senegal 9/28/60, Serbia and Montenegro 11/1/00, Seychelles 9/21/76, Sierra Leone 9/27/61, Singapore 9/21/65, Slovakia 1/19/93, Slovenia 5/22/92, Solomon Islands 9/19/78, Somalia 9/20/60, South Africa 11/7/45, Spain 12/14/55, Sri Lanka 12/14/55, Sudan 11/12/56, Suriname 12/4/75, Swaziland 9/24/68, Sweden 11/19/46, Switzerland 9/10/02, Syrian Arab Republic 10/24/45, Tajikistan 3/2/92, Thailand 12/16/46, Timor-Leste 9/27/02, Togo 9/20/60, Tonga 9/14/99, Trinidad and Tobago 9/18/62, Tunisia 11/12/56, Turkey 10/24/45, Turkmenistan 3/2/92, Tuvalu 9/5/00, Uganda 10/25/62, Ukraine 10/24/45, United Arab Emirates 12/9/71, United Kingdom of Great Britain and Northern Ireland 10/24/45, United Republic of Tanzania (formerly Tanganyika and Zanzibar) 12/14/61,

United States of America 10/24/45, Uruguay 12/18/45, Uzbekistan 3/2/92, Vanuatu 9/15/81, Venezuela 11/15/45, Vietnam 9/20/77, Yemen 9/30/47, Zambia 12/1/64, Zimbabwe (formerly Rhodesia) 8/25/80

SWITZERLAND IS THE newest member of the UN. Neutral since 1815, it joined the world body in 2002.

91 What are the two major parties in America today?

☞ *Democratic and Republican*

92 What type of government do we have?

☞ *Republican*

ACCORDING TO ARTICLE IV, Section 4, of the Constitution, the United States shall guarantee to every state in the Union a republican form of government.

REPUBLIC: A STATE or nation in which the supreme power rests in all the citizens entitled to vote. This power is exercised by representatives elected, directly or indirectly, by them and responsible to them.

DEMOCRACY: A WAY of governing a country in which the people elect representatives to form a government on their behalf. A country with such a government embraces the idea that everyone in that country has equal rights.

APPENDIX A

The Declaration of Independence

··

IN CONGRESS, July 4, 1776.

The unanimous Declaration of the thirteen united States of America,

When in the Course of human events, it becomes necessary for one people to dissolve the political bands which have connected them with another, and to assume among the powers of the earth, the separate and equal station to which the Laws of Nature and of Nature's God entitle them, a decent respect to the opinions of mankind requires that they should declare the causes which impel them to the separation.

We hold these truths to be self-evident, that all men are created equal, that they are endowed by their Creator with certain unalienable Rights, that among these are Life, Liberty and the pursuit of Happiness.——That to secure these rights, Governments are instituted among Men, deriving their just powers from the consent of the governed,——That whenever any Form of Government becomes destructive of these ends, it is the Right of the People to alter or to abolish it, and to institute a new Government, laying its foundation on such principles and organizing its powers in such form, as to them shall seem most likely to effect their Safety and Happiness. Prudence, indeed, will dictate that Governments long established should not be changed for light and transient causes; and accordingly all experience hath shewn, that mankind are more disposed to suffer, while evils are sufferable, than to right themselves by abolishing the forms to which they are accustomed. But when a long train of abuses and usurpations, pursuing invariably the same Object evinces a design to reduce them under absolute Despotism, it is their right, it is their duty, to throw off such Government, and to provide new Guards for their future security.——Such has been the patient sufferance of these Colonies; and such is now the necessity which constrains them to alter their former Systems of Government. The history of the present King of Great Britain is a history of repeated injuries and usurpations, all having in direct object the establishment of an absolute Tyranny over these States. To prove this, let Facts be submitted to a candid world.

He has refused his Assent to Laws, the most wholesome and necessary for the public good.

He has forbidden his Governors to pass Laws of immediate and pressing importance, unless suspended in their operation till his Assent should be obtained; and when so suspended, he has utterly neglected to attend to them.

He has refused to pass other Laws for the accommodation of large districts of people, unless those people would relinquish the right of Representation in the Legislature, a right inestimable to them and formidable to tyrants only.

He has called together legislative bodies at places unusual, uncomfortable, and distant from the depository of their public Records, for the sole purpose of fatiguing them into compliance with his measures.

He has dissolved Representative Houses repeatedly, for opposing with manly firmness his invasions on the rights of the people.

He has refused for a long time, after such dissolutions, to cause others to be elected; whereby the Legislative powers, incapable of Annihilation, have returned to the People at large for their exercise; the State remaining in the mean time exposed to all the dangers of invasion from without, and convulsions within.

He has endeavoured to prevent the population of these States; for that purpose obstructing the Laws for Naturalization of Foreigners; refusing to pass others to encourage their migrations hither, and raising the conditions of new Appropriations of Lands.

He has obstructed the Administration of Justice, by refusing his Assent to Laws for establishing Judiciary powers.

He has made Judges dependent on his Will alone, for the tenure of their offices, and the amount and payment of their salaries.

He has erected a multitude of New Offices, and sent hither swarms of Officers to harrass our people, and eat out their substance.

He has kept among us, in times of peace, Standing Armies without the Consent of our legislatures.

He has affected to render the Military independent of and superior to the Civil power.

He has combined with others to subject us to a jurisdiction foreign to our constitution, and unacknowledged by our laws; giving his Assent to their Acts of pretended Legislation:

For Quartering large bodies of armed troops among us;

For protecting them, by a mock Trial, from punishment for any Murders which they should commit on the Inhabitants of these States;

For cutting off our Trade with all parts of the world;

For imposing Taxes on us without our Consent;

For depriving us in many cases, of the benefits of Trial by Jury;

For transporting us beyond Seas to be tried for pretended offences;

For abolishing the free System of English Laws in a neighbouring Province, establishing therein an Arbitrary government, and enlarging its Boundaries so as to render it at once an example and fit instrument for introducing the same absolute rule into these Colonies;

For taking away our Charters, abolishing our most valuable Laws, and altering fundamentally the Forms of our Governments;

For suspending our own Legislatures, and declaring themselves invested with power to legislate for us in all cases whatsoever.

He has abdicated Government here, by declaring us out of his Protection and waging War against us.

He has plundered our seas, ravaged our Coasts, burnt our towns, and destroyed the lives of our people.

He is at this time transporting large Armies of foreign Mercenaries to compleat the works of death, desolation and tyranny, already begun with circumstances of Cruelty & perfidy scarcely paralleled in the most barbarous ages, and totally unworthy the Head of a civilized nation.

He has constrained our fellow Citizens taken Captive on the high Seas to bear Arms against their Country, to become the executioners of their friends and Brethren, or to fall themselves by their Hands.

He has excited domestic insurrections amongst us, and has endeavoured to bring on the inhabitants of our frontiers, the merciless Indian Savages, whose known rule of warfare, is an undistinguished destruction of all ages, sexes and conditions.

In every stage of these Oppressions We have Petitioned for Redress in the most humble terms: Our repeated Petitions have been answered only by repeated injury. A Prince whose character is thus marked by every act which may define a Tyrant, is unfit to be the ruler of a free people.

Nor have We been wanting in attentions to our British brethren. We have warned them from time to time of attempts by their legislature to extend an unwarrantable jurisdiction over us. We have reminded them of the circumstances of our emigration and settlement here. We have appealed to their native justice and magnanimity, and we have conjured them by the ties of our common kindred to disavow these usurpations, which would inevitably interrupt our connections and correspondence. They too have been deaf to the voice of justice and of consanguinity. We must, therefore, acquiesce in the necessity, which denounces our Separation, and hold them, as we hold the rest of mankind, Enemies in War, in Peace Friends.

We, therefore, the Representatives of the united States of America, in General Congress, Assembled, appealing to the Supreme Judge of the world for the rectitude of our intentions, do, in the Name, and by Authority of the good People of these Colonies, solemnly publish and declare, That these United Colonies are, and of Right ought to be Free and Independent States; that they are Absolved from all Allegiance to the British Crown, and that all political connection between them and the State of Great Britain, is and ought to be totally dissolved; and that as Free and Independent States, they have full Power to levy War, conclude Peace, contract Alliances, establish Commerce, and to do all other Acts and Things which Independent States may of right do. And for the support of this Declaration, with a firm reliance on the protection of divine Providence, we mutually pledge to each other our Lives, our Fortunes and our sacred Honor.

The 56 signatures on the Declaration appear in the positions indicated:

Column 1

GEORGIA
Button Gwinnett
Lyman Hall
George Walton

Column 2

NORTH CAROLINA
William Hooper
Joseph Hewes
John Penn

SOUTH CAROLINA
Edward Rutledge

Thomas Heyward, Jr.
Thomas Lynch, Jr.
Arthur Middleton

Column 3

MASSACHUSETTS
John Hancock

MARYLAND
Samuel Chase
William Paca
Thomas Stone
Charles Carroll of
  Carrollton

VIRGINIA
George Wythe
Richard Henry Lee
Thomas Jefferson
Benjamin Harrison
Thomas Nelson, Jr.
Francis Lightfoot Lee
Carter Braxton

Column 4

PENNSYLVANIA
Robert Morris
Benjamin Rush
Benjamin Franklin
John Morton
George Clymer
James Smith
George Taylor
James Wilson
George Ross

DELAWARE
Caesar Rodney
George Read
Thomas McKean

Column 5

NEW YORK
William Floyd
Philip Livingston

Francis Lewis
Lewis Morris

NEW JERSEY
Richard Stockton
John Witherspoon
Francis Hopkinson
John Hart
Abraham Clark

Column 6

NEW HAMPSHIRE
Josiah Bartlett
William Whipple

MASSACHUSETTS
Samuel Adams
John Adams
Robert Treat Paine
Elbridge Gerry

RHODE ISLAND
Stephen Hopkins
William Ellery

CONNECTICUT
Roger Sherman
Samuel Huntington
William Williams
Oliver Wolcott

NEW HAMPSHIRE
Matthew Thornton

APPENDIX B

The U.S. Constitution

••

[NOTE: Italicized sections or clauses were later superseded by amendments.]

WE THE PEOPLE of the United States, in Order to form a more perfect Union, establish Justice, insure domestic Tranquility, provide for the common defense, promote the general Welfare, and secure the Blessings of Liberty to ourselves and our Posterity, do ordain and establish this Constitution for the United States of America.

••

Article I

Section 1
All legislative Powers herein granted shall be vested in a Congress of the United States, which shall consist of a Senate and House of Representatives.

Section 2
1. The House of Representatives shall be composed of Members chosen every second Year by the People of the several States, and the Electors in each State shall have the Qualifications requisite for Electors of the most numerous Branch of the State Legislature.

2. No Person shall be a Representative who shall not have attained to the Age of twenty five Years, and been seven Years a Citizen of the United States, and who shall not, when elected, be an Inhabitant of that State in which he shall be chosen.

3. *Representatives and direct Taxes shall be apportioned among the several States which may be included within this Union, according to their respective Numbers, which shall be determined by adding to the whole Number of free Persons, including those bound to Service for a Term of Years, and excluding Indians not taxed, three fifths of all other Persons.* The actual Enumeration shall be made within three Years after the first Meeting of the Congress of the United States, and within every subsequent Term of ten Years, in such Manner as they shall by Law direct. The Number of Representatives shall not exceed one for every thirty Thousand, but each State shall have at Least one Representative; and until such enumeration shall be made, the State of New Hampshire shall be entitled to choose three, Massachusetts eight, Rhode Island and Providence Plantations one, Connecticut five, New York six, New Jersey four, Pennsylvania eight, Delaware one, Maryland six, Virginia ten, North Carolina five, South Carolina five, and Georgia three.

4. When vacancies happen in the Representation from any State, the Executive Authority thereof shall issue Writs of Election to fill such Vacancies.

5. The House of Representatives shall choose their Speaker and other Officers; and shall have the sole Power of Impeachment.

Section 3

1. The Senate of the United States shall be composed of two Senators from each State, *chosen by the Legislature* thereof for six Years; and each Senator shall have one Vote.

2. Immediately after they shall be assembled in Consequence of the first Election, they shall be divided as equally as may be into three Classes. The Seats of the Senators of the first Class shall be vacated at the Expiration of the second Year, of the second Class at the Expiration of the fourth Year, and of the third Class at the Expiration of the sixth Year, so that one third may be chosen every second Year; *and if Vacancies happen by Resignation, or otherwise, during the Recess of the Legislature of any State, the Executive thereof may make temporary Appointments until the next Meeting of the Legislature, which shall then fill such Vacancies.*

3. No Person shall be a Senator who shall not have attained to the Age of thirty Years, and been nine Years a Citizen of the United States, and who shall not, when elected, be an Inhabitant of that State for which he shall be chosen.

4. The Vice President of the United States shall be President of the Senate, but shall have no Vote, unless they be equally divided.

5. The Senate shall choose their other Officers, and also a President pro tempore, in the Absence of the Vice President, or when he shall exercise the Office of President of the United States.

6. The Senate shall have the sole Power to try all Impeachments. When sitting for that Purpose, they shall be on Oath

or Affirmation. When the President of the United States is tried, the Chief Justice shall preside: And no Person shall be convicted without the Concurrence of two thirds of the Members present.

7. Judgment in Cases of Impeachment shall not extend further than to removal from Office, and disqualification to hold and enjoy any Office of honor, Trust or Profit under the United States: but the Party convicted shall nevertheless be liable and subject to Indictment, Trial, Judgment and Punishment, according to Law.

Section 4
1. The Times, Places and Manner of holding Elections for Senators and Representatives shall be prescribed in each State by the Legislature thereof; but the Congress may at any time by Law make or alter such Regulations, except as to the Places of choosing Senators.

2. The Congress shall assemble at least once in every Year, and such Meeting shall *be on the first Monday in December*, unless they shall by Law appoint a different Day.

Section 5
1. Each House shall be the Judge of the Elections, Returns and Qualifications of its own Members, and a Majority of each shall constitute a Quorum to do Business; but a smaller Number may adjourn from day to day, and may be authorized to compel the Attendance of absent Members, in such Manner, and under such Penalties as each House may provide.

2. Each House may determine the Rules of its Proceedings, punish its Members for disorderly Behaviour, and, with the Concurrence of two thirds, expel a Member.

3. Each House shall keep a Journal of its Proceedings, and from time to time publish the same, excepting such Parts as may in their Judgment require Secrecy; and the Yeas and Nays of the Members of either House on any question shall, at the Desire of one fifth of those Present, be entered on the Journal.

4. Neither House, during the Session of Congress, shall, without the Consent of the other, adjourn for more than three days, nor to any other Place than that in which the two Houses shall be sitting.

Section 6
1. The Senators and Representatives shall receive a Compensation for their Services, to be ascertained by Law, and paid out of the Treasury of the United States. They shall in all Cases, except Treason, Felony and Breach of the Peace, be privileged from Arrest during their Attendance at the Session of their respective Houses, and in going to and returning from the same; and for any Speech or Debate in either House, they shall not be questioned in any other Place.

2. No Senator or Representative shall, during the Time for which he was elected, be appointed to any civil Office under the Authority of the United States, which shall have been created, or the Emoluments whereof shall have been increased during such time; and no Person holding any Of-

fice under the United States, shall be a Member of either House during his Continuance in Office.

Section 7

1. All Bills for raising Revenue shall originate in the House of Representatives; but the Senate may propose or concur with Amendments as on other Bills.

2. Every Bill which shall have passed the House of Representatives and the Senate, shall, before it become a Law, be presented to the President of the United States: If he approve he shall sign it, but if not he shall return it, with his Objections to that House in which it shall have originated, who shall enter the Objections at large on their Journal, and proceed to reconsider it. If after such Reconsideration two thirds of that House shall agree to pass the Bill, it shall be sent, together with the Objections, to the other House, by which it shall likewise be reconsidered, and if approved by two thirds of that House, it shall become a Law. But in all such Cases the Votes of both Houses shall be determined by yeas and Nays, and the Names of the Persons voting for and against the Bill shall be entered on the Journal of each House respectively. If any Bill shall not be returned by the President within ten Days (Sundays excepted) after it shall have been presented to him, the Same shall be a Law, in like Manner as if he had signed it, unless the Congress by their Adjournment prevent its Return, in which Case it shall not be a Law.

3. Every Order, Resolution, or Vote to which the Concurrence of the Senate and House of Representatives may be necessary (except on a question of Adjournment) shall be presented to the President of the United States; and before

the Same shall take Effect, shall be approved by him, or being disapproved by him, shall be repassed by two thirds of the Senate and House of Representatives, according to the Rules and Limitations prescribed in the Case of a Bill.

Section 8
The Congress shall have Power

1. To lay and collect Taxes, Duties, Imposts and Excises, to pay the Debts and provide for the common Defence and general Welfare of the United States; but all Duties, Imposts and Excises shall be uniform throughout the United States;

2. To borrow Money on the credit of the United States;

3. To regulate Commerce with foreign Nations, and among the several States, and with the Indian Tribes;

4. To establish a uniform Rule of Naturalization, and uniform Laws on the subject of Bankruptcies throughout the United States;

5. To coin Money, regulate the Value thereof, and of foreign Coin, and fix the Standard of Weights and Measures;

6. To provide for the Punishment of counterfeiting the Securities and current Coin of the United States;

7. To establish Post Offices and post Roads;

8. To promote the Progress of Science and useful Arts, by securing for limited Times to Authors and Inventors the exclusive Right to their respective Writings and Discoveries;

9. To constitute Tribunals inferior to the supreme Court;

10. To define and punish Piracies and Felonies committed on the high Seas, and Offences against the Law of Nations;

11. To declare War, grant Letters of Marque and Reprisal, and make Rules concerning Captures on Land and Water;

12. To raise and support Armies, but no Appropriation of Money to that Use shall be for a longer Term than two Years;

13. To provide and maintain a Navy;

14. To make Rules for the Government and Regulation of the land and naval Forces;

15. To provide for calling forth the Militia to execute the Laws of the Union, suppress Insurrections and repel Invasions;

16. To provide for organizing, arming, and disciplining, the Militia, and for governing such Part of them as may be employed in the Service of the United States, reserving to the States respectively, the Appointment of the Officers, and the Authority of training the Militia according to the discipline prescribed by Congress;

17. To exercise exclusive Legislation in all Cases whatsoever, over such District (not exceeding ten Miles square) as may, by Cession of particular States, and the Acceptance of Congress, become the Seat of the Government of the United States, and to exercise like Authority over all Places purchased by the Consent of the Legislature of the State in which the Same shall be, for the Erection of Forts,

Magazines, Arsenals, dock-Yards, and other needful Buildings;—And

18. To make all Laws which shall be necessary and proper for carrying into Execution the foregoing Powers, and all other Powers vested by this Constitution in the Government of the United States, or in any Department or Officer thereof.

Section 9
1. The Migration or Importation of such Persons as any of the States now existing shall think proper to admit, shall not be prohibited by the Congress prior to the Year one thousand eight hundred and eight, but a Tax or duty may be imposed on such Importation, not exceeding ten dollars for each Person.

2. The Privilege of the Writ of Habeas Corpus shall not be suspended, unless when in Cases of Rebellion or Invasion the public Safety may require it.

3. No Bill of Attainder or ex post facto Law shall be passed.

4. No Capitation, or other direct, Tax shall be laid, *unless in Proportion to the Census or enumeration herein before directed to be taken.*

5. No Tax or Duty shall be laid on Articles exported from any State.

6. No Preference shall be given by any Regulation of Commerce or Revenue to the Ports of one State over those of another; nor shall Vessels bound to, or from, one State, be obliged to enter, clear, or pay Duties in another.

7. No Money shall be drawn from the Treasury, but in Consequence of Appropriations made by Law; and a regular Statement and Account of the Receipts and Expenditures of all public Money shall be published from time to time.

8. No Title of Nobility shall be granted by the United States: And no Person holding any Office of Profit or Trust under them, shall, without the Consent of the Congress, accept of any present, Emolument, Office, or Title, of any kind whatever, from any King, Prince, or foreign State.

Section 10

1. No State shall enter into any Treaty, Alliance, or Confederation; grant Letters of Marque and Reprisal; coin Money; emit Bills of Credit; make any Thing but gold and silver Coin a Tender in Payment of Debts; pass any Bill of Attainder, ex post facto Law, or Law impairing the Obligation of Contracts, or grant any Title of Nobility.

2. No State shall, without the Consent of the Congress, lay any Imposts or Duties on Imports or Exports, except what may be absolutely necessary for executing its inspection Laws: and the net Produce of all Duties and Imposts, laid by any State on Imports or Exports, shall be for the Use of the Treasury of the United States; and all such Laws shall be subject to the Revision and Controul of the Congress.

3. No State shall, without the Consent of Congress, lay any Duty of Tonnage, keep Troops, or Ships of War in time of Peace, enter into any Agreement or Compact with another State, or with a foreign Power, or engage in War, unless actually invaded, or in such imminent Danger as will not admit of delay.

Article II

Section 1

1. The executive Power shall be vested in a President of the United States of America. He shall hold his Office during the Term of four Years, and, together with the Vice President, chosen for the same Term, be elected, as follows:

2. Each State shall appoint, in such Manner as the Legislature thereof may direct, a Number of Electors, equal to the whole Number of Senators and Representatives to which the State may be entitled in the Congress: but no Senator or Representative, or Person holding an Office of Trust or Profit under the United States, shall be appointed an Elector.

3. *The Electors shall meet in their respective States, and vote by Ballot for two Persons, of whom one at least shall not be an Inhabitant of the same State with themselves. And they shall make a List of all the Persons voted for, and of the Number of Votes for each; which List they shall sign and certify, and transmit sealed to the Seat of the Government of the United States, directed to the President of the Senate. The President of the Senate shall, in the Presence of the Senate and House of Representatives, open all the Certificates, and the Votes shall then be counted. The Person having the greatest Number of Votes shall be the President, if such Number be a Majority of the whole Number of Electors appointed; and if there be more than one who have such Majority, and have an equal Number of Votes, then the House of Representatives shall immediately choose by Ballot one of them for President; and if no Person have a Majority, then from the five highest on the List the said House shall in like Manner choose the President. But in choosing*

the President, the Votes shall be taken by States, the Representation from each State having one Vote; A quorum for this purpose shall consist of a Member or Members from two thirds of the States, and a Majority of all the States shall be necessary to a Choice. In every Case, after the Choice of the President, the Person having the greatest Number of Votes of the Electors shall be the Vice President. But if there should remain two or more who have equal Votes, the Senate shall choose from them by Ballot the Vice President.

4. The Congress may determine the Time of choosing the Electors, and the Day on which they shall give their Votes; which Day shall be the same throughout the United States.

5. No Person except a natural born Citizen, or a Citizen of the United States, at the time of the Adoption of this Constitution, shall be eligible to the Office of President; neither shall any Person be eligible to that Office who shall not have attained to the Age of thirty five Years, and been fourteen Years a Resident within the United States.

6. In Case of the Removal of the President from Office, or of his Death, Resignation, or Inability to discharge the Powers and Duties of the said Office, the Same shall devolve on the Vice President, and the Congress may by Law provide for the Case of Removal, Death, Resignation, or Inability, both of the President and Vice President, declaring what Officer shall then act as President, and such Officer shall act accordingly, until the Disability be removed, or a President shall be elected.

7. The President shall, at stated Times, receive for his Services, a Compensation, which shall neither be increased nor diminished during the Period for which he shall have been

elected, and he shall not receive within that Period any other Emolument from the United States, or any of them.

8. Before he enter on the Execution of his Office, he shall take the following Oath or Affirmation: —"I do solemnly swear (or affirm) that I will faithfully execute the Office of President of the United States, and will to the best of my Ability, preserve, protect and defend the Constitution of the United States."

Section 2

1. The President shall be Commander in Chief of the Army and Navy of the United States, and of the Militia of the several States, when called into the actual Service of the United States; he may require the Opinion, in writing, of the principal Officer in each of the executive Departments, upon any Subject relating to the Duties of their respective Offices, and he shall have Power to grant Reprieves and Pardons for Offences against the United States, except in Cases of Impeachment.

2. He shall have Power, by and with the Advice and Consent of the Senate, to make Treaties, provided two thirds of the Senators present concur; and he shall nominate, and by and with the Advice and Consent of the Senate, shall appoint Ambassadors, other public Ministers and Consuls, Judges of the supreme Court, and all other Officers of the United States, whose Appointments are not herein otherwise provided for, and which shall be established by Law: but the Congress may by Law vest the Appointment of such inferior Officers, as they think proper, in the

President alone, in the Courts of Law, or in the Heads of Departments.

3. The President shall have Power to fill up all Vacancies that may happen during the Recess of the Senate, by granting Commissions which shall expire at the End of their next Session.

Section 3
He shall from time to time give to the Congress Information of the State of the Union, and recommend to their Consideration such Measures as he shall judge necessary and expedient; he may, on extraordinary Occasions, convene both Houses, or either of them, and in Case of Disagreement between them, with Respect to the Time of Adjournment, he may adjourn them to such Time as he shall think proper; he shall receive Ambassadors and other public Ministers; he shall take Care that the Laws be faithfully executed, and shall Commission all the Officers of the United States.

Section 4
The President, Vice President and all civil Officers of the United States, shall be removed from Office on Impeachment for, and Conviction of, Treason, Bribery, or other high Crimes and Misdemeanors.

Article III
Section 1
The judicial Power of the United States shall be vested in one supreme Court, and in such inferior Courts as the

Congress may from time to time ordain and establish. The Judges, both of the supreme and inferior Courts, shall hold their Offices during good Behaviour, and shall, at stated Times, receive for their Services a Compensation, which shall not be diminished during their Continuance in Office.

Section 2
1. The judicial Power shall extend to all Cases, in Law and Equity, arising under this Constitution, the Laws of the United States, and Treaties made, or which shall be made, under their Authority;—to all Cases affecting Ambassadors, other public Ministers and Consuls;—to all Cases of admiralty and maritime Jurisdiction;—to Controversies to which the United States shall be a Party;—to Controversies between two or more States;—*between a State and Citizens of another State*;—between Citizens of different States;—between Citizens of the same State claiming Lands under Grants of different States, and between a State, or the Citizens thereof, and foreign States, Citizens or Subjects.

2. In all Cases affecting Ambassadors, other public Ministers and Consuls, and those in which a State shall be Party, the supreme Court shall have original Jurisdiction. In all the other Cases before mentioned, the supreme Court shall have appellate Jurisdiction, both as to Law and Fact, with such Exceptions, and under such Regulations as the Congress shall make.

3. The Trial of all Crimes, except in Cases of Impeachment, shall be by Jury; and such Trial shall be held in the State where the said Crimes shall have been committed;

but when not committed within any State, the Trial shall be at such Place or Places as the Congress may by Law have directed.

Section 3

1. Treason against the United States, shall consist only in levying War against them, or in adhering to their Enemies, giving them Aid and Comfort. No Person shall be convicted of Treason unless on the Testimony of two Witnesses to the same overt Act, or on Confession in open Court.

2. The Congress shall have Power to declare the Punishment of Treason, but no Attainder of Treason shall work Corruption of Blood, or Forfeiture except during the Life of the Person attained.

Article IV

Section 1

Full Faith and Credit shall be given in each State to the public Acts, Records, and judicial Proceedings of every other State. And the Congress may by general Laws prescribe the Manner in which such Acts, Records and Proceedings shall be proved, and the Effect thereof.

Section 2

1. The Citizens of each State shall be entitled to all Privileges and Immunities of Citizens in the several States.

2. A Person charged in any State with Treason, Felony, or other Crime, who shall flee from Justice, and be found in another State, shall on Demand of the executive Au-

thority of the State from which he fled, be delivered up, to be removed to the State having Jurisdiction of the Crime.

3. *No Person held to Service or Labour in one State, under the Laws thereof, escaping into another, shall, in Consequence of any Law or Regulation therein, be discharged from such Service or Labour, but shall be delivered up on Claim of the Party to whom such Service or Labour may be due.*

Section 3
1. New States may be admitted by the Congress into this Union; but no new State shall be formed or erected within the Jurisdiction of any other State; nor any State be formed by the Junction of two or more States, or Parts of States, without the Consent of the Legislatures of the States concerned as well as of the Congress.

2. The Congress shall have Power to dispose of and make all needful Rules and Regulations respecting the Territory or other Property belonging to the United States; and nothing in this Constitution shall be so construed as to Prejudice any Claims of the United States, or of any particular State.

Section 4
The United States shall guarantee to every State in this Union a Republican Form of Government, and shall protect each of them against Invasion; and on Application of the Legislature, or of the Executive (when the Legislature cannot be convened), against domestic Violence.

Article V

The Congress, whenever two thirds of both Houses shall deem it necessary, shall propose Amendments to this Constitution, or, on the Application of the Legislatures of two thirds of the several States, shall call a Convention for proposing Amendments, which, in either Case, shall be valid to all Intents and Purposes, as Part of this Constitution, when ratified by the Legislatures of three fourths of the several States, or by Conventions in three fourths thereof, as the one or the other Mode of Ratification may be proposed by the Congress; Provided that no Amendment which may be made prior to the Year One thousand eight hundred and eight shall in any Manner affect the first and fourth Clauses in the Ninth Section of the first Article; and that no State, without its Consent, shall be deprived of its equal Suffrage in the Senate.

Article VI

1. All Debts contracted and Engagements entered into, before the Adoption of this Constitution, shall be as valid against the United States under this Constitution, as under the Confederation.

2. This Constitution, and the Laws of the United States which shall be made in Pursuance thereof; and all Treaties made, or which shall be made, under the Authority of the United States, shall be the supreme Law of the Land; and the Judges in every State shall be bound thereby, any Thing in the Constitution or Laws of any State to the Contrary notwithstanding.

3. The Senators and Representatives before mentioned, and the Members of the several State Legislatures, and all executive and judicial Officers, both of the United States and of the several States, shall be bound by Oath or Affirmation, to support this Constitution; but no religious Test shall ever be required as a Qualification to any Office or public Trust under the United States.

Article VII

The Ratification of the Conventions of nine States, shall be sufficient for the Establishment of this Constitution between the States so ratifying the Same.

Done in Convention by the Unanimous Consent of the States present the Seventeenth Day of September in the Year of our Lord one thousand seven hundred and Eighty seven and of the Independence of the United States of America the Twelfth. In witness whereof We have hereunto subscribed our Names,

G°.Washington
Presidt. and deputy from Virginia

DELAWARE
Geo: Read
Gunning Bedford jun.
John Dickinson
Richard Bassett
Jaco: Broom

MARYLAND
James McHenry
Dan of St Thos. Jenifer
Danl. Carroll

VIRGINIA
John Blair
James Madison Jr.

NORTH CAROLINA
Wm. Blount
Richd. Dobbs Spaight
Hu Williamson

SOUTH CAROLINA
J. Rutledge
Charles Cotesworth Pinckney
Charles Pinckney
Pierce Butler

GEORGIA
William Few
Abr Baldwin

NEW HAMPSHIRE
John Langdon
Nicholas Gilman

MASSACHUSETTS
Nathaniel Gorham
Rufus King

CONNECTICUT
Wm. Saml. Johnson
Roger Sherman

NEW YORK
Alexander Hamilton

NEW JERSEY
Wil: Livingston
David Brearley
Wm. Paterson
Jona: Dayton

PENNSYLVANIA
B. Franklin
Thomas Mifflin
Robt. Morris
Geo. Clymer
Thos. FitzSimons
Jared Ingersoll
James Wilson
Gouv Morris

The Bill of Rights

....

Note: The following text is a transcription of the first ten Amendments to the Constitution in their original form. These Amendments were ratified December 15, 1791, and form what is known as the "Bill of Rights."

Amendment I

Congress shall make no law respecting an establishment of religion, or prohibiting the free exercise thereof; or abridging the freedom of speech, or of the press; or the right of the people peaceably to assemble, and to petition the Government for a redress of grievances.

Amendment II

A well regulated Militia, being necessary to the security of a free State, the right of the people to keep and bear Arms, shall not be infringed.

Amendment III

No Soldier shall, in time of peace be quartered in any house, without the consent of the Owner, nor in time of war, but in a manner to be prescribed by law.

Amendment IV

The right of the people to be secure in their persons, houses, papers, and effects, against unreasonable searches and seizures, shall not be violated, and no Warrants shall issue, but upon probable cause, supported by Oath or affirmation, and particularly describing the place to be searched, and the persons or things to be seized.

Amendment V

No person shall be held to answer for a capital, or otherwise infamous crime, unless on a presentment or indictment of a Grand Jury, except in cases arising in the land or naval forces, or in the Militia, when in actual service in time of War or public danger; nor shall any person be subject for the same offence to be twice put in jeopardy of life or limb; nor shall be compelled in any criminal case to be a witness against himself, nor be deprived of life, liberty, or property, without due process of law; nor shall private property be taken for public use, without just compensation.

Amendment VI

In all criminal prosecutions, the accused shall enjoy the right to a speedy and public trial, by an impartial jury of the State and district wherein the crime shall have been committed, which district shall have been previously ascertained by law, and to be informed of the nature and cause of the accusation; to be confronted with the witnesses against him; to have compulsory process for obtaining witnesses in his favor, and to have the Assistance of Counsel for his defence.

Amendment VII

In Suits at common law, where the value in controversy shall exceed twenty dollars, the right of trial by jury shall be preserved, and no fact tried by a jury, shall be otherwise re-examined in any Court of the United States, than according to the rules of the common law.

Amendment VIII

Excessive bail shall not be required, nor excessive fines imposed, nor cruel and unusual punishments inflicted.

Amendment IX

The enumeration in the Constitution, of certain rights, shall not be construed to deny or disparage others retained by the people.

Amendment X

The powers not delegated to the United States by the Constitution, nor prohibited by it to the States, are reserved to the States respectively, or to the people.

Amendments XI–XXVII

••

Constitutional Amendments I–X make up what is known as the *Bill of Rights*. Amendments XI–XXVII are listed below.

Amendment XI

Passed by Congress March 4, 1794. Ratified February 7, 1795.

Note: Article III, Section 2, of the Constitution was modified by the Eleventh Amendment.

The Judicial power of the United States shall not be construed to extend to any suit in law or equity, commenced or prosecuted against one of the United States by Citizens of another State, or by Citizens or Subjects of any Foreign State.

Amendment XII

Passed by Congress December 9, 1803. Ratified June 15, 1804.

Note: A portion of Article II, Section 1 of the Constitution was superseded by the Twelfth Amendment.

The Electors shall meet in their respective states and vote by ballot for President and Vice-President, one of whom, at least, shall not be an inhabitant of the same state with themselves; they shall name in their ballots the person voted for as President, and in distinct ballots the person voted for as Vice-President, and they shall make distinct lists of all persons voted for as President, and of all persons voted for as Vice-President, and of the number of votes for each, which lists they shall sign and certify, and transmit sealed to the seat of the government of the United States, directed to the President of the Senate;—the President of the Senate shall, in the presence of the Senate and House of Representatives, open all the certificates and the votes shall then be counted;—The person having the greatest number of votes for President, shall be the President, if such number be a majority of the whole number of Electors appointed; and if no person have such majority, then from the persons having the highest numbers not exceeding three on the list of those voted for as President, the House of Representatives shall choose immediately, by ballot, the President. But in choosing the President, the votes shall be taken by states, the representation from each state having one vote; a quorum for this purpose shall consist of a member or members from two-thirds of the states, and a majority of all the states shall be necessary to a choice. [And if the House of Representatives shall not choose a President whenever the right of choice shall devolve upon them, before the fourth day of March next following, then the Vice-President shall act as President, as in case of the death or other constitutional disability of the President.—]* The person having the greatest number of votes as Vice-President, shall be the Vice-President, if such number be a majority of the whole number of

*Superseded by Section 3 of the Twentieth Amendment.

Electors appointed, and if no person have a majority, then from the two highest numbers on the list, the Senate shall choose the Vice-President; a quorum for the purpose shall consist of two-thirds of the whole number of Senators, and a majority of the whole number shall be necessary to a choice. But no person constitutionally ineligible to the office of President shall be eligible to that of Vice-President of the United States.

Amendment XIII

Passed by Congress January 31, 1865. Ratified December 18, 1865.

Note: A portion of Article IV, Section 2, of the Constitution was superseded by the Thirteenth Amendment.

Section 1
Neither slavery nor involuntary servitude, except as a punishment for crime whereof the party shall have been duly convicted, shall exist within the United States, or any place subject to their jurisdiction.

Section 2
Congress shall have power to enforce this article by appropriate legislation.

Amendment XIV

Passed by Congress June 13, 1866. Ratified July 9, 1868.

Note: Article I, Section 2, of the Constitution was modified by Section 2 of the Fourteenth Amendment.

Section 1

All persons born or naturalized in the United States, and subject to the jurisdiction thereof, are citizens of the United States and of the State wherein they reside. No State shall make or enforce any law which shall abridge the privileges or immunities of citizens of the United States; nor shall any State deprive any person of life, liberty, or property, without due process of law; nor deny to any person within its jurisdiction the equal protection of the laws.

Section 2

Representatives shall be apportioned among the several States according to their respective numbers, counting the whole number of persons in each State, excluding Indians not taxed. But when the right to vote at any election for the choice of electors for President and Vice-President of the United States, Representatives in Congress, the Executive and Judicial officers of a State, or the members of the Legislature thereof, is denied to any of the male inhabitants of such State, being twenty-one years of age,* and citizens of the United States, or in any way abridged, except for participation in rebellion, or other crime, the basis of representation therein shall be reduced in the proportion which the number of such male citizens shall bear to the whole number of male citizens twenty-one years of age in such State.

Section 3

No person shall be a Senator or Representative in Congress, or elector of President and Vice-President, or hold

*Changed by Section 1 of the Twenty-sixth Amendment.

any office, civil or military, under the United States, or under any State, who, having previously taken an oath, as a member of Congress, or as an officer of the United States, or as a member of any State legislature, or as an executive or judicial officer of any State, to support the Constitution of the United States, shall have engaged in insurrection or rebellion against the same, or given aid or comfort to the enemies thereof. But Congress may by a vote of two-thirds of each House, remove such disability.

Section 4
The validity of the public debt of the United States, authorized by law, including debts incurred for payment of pensions and bounties for services in suppressing insurrection or rebellion, shall not be questioned. But neither the United States nor any State shall assume or pay any debt or obligation incurred in aid of insurrection or rebellion against the United States, or any claim for the loss or emancipation of any slave; but all such debts, obligations and claims shall be held illegal and void.

Section 5
The Congress shall have the power to enforce, by appropriate legislation, the provisions of this article.

Amendment XV

Passed by Congress February 26, 1869. Ratified February 3, 1870.

Section 1
The right of citizens of the United States to vote shall not be denied or abridged by the United States or by any

State on account of race, color, or previous condition of servitude.

Section 2
The Congress shall have the power to enforce this article by appropriate legislation.

Amendment XVI

Passed by Congress July 2, 1909. Ratified February 3, 1913.

Note: Article I, Section 9, of the Constitution was modified by the Sixteenth Amendment.

The Congress shall have power to lay and collect taxes on incomes, from whatever source derived, without apportionment among the several States, and without regard to any census or enumeration.

Amendment XVII

Passed by Congress May 13, 1912. Ratified April 8, 1913.

Note: Article I, Section 3, of the Constitution was modified by the Seventeenth Amendment.

The Senate of the United States shall be composed of two Senators from each State, elected by the people thereof, for six years; and each Senator shall have one vote. The electors in each State shall have the qualifications requisite for electors of the most numerous branch of the State legislatures.

When vacancies happen in the representation of any State in the Senate, the executive authority of such State shall issue writs of election to fill such vacancies: *Provided*, That the legislature of any State may empower the executive thereof to make temporary appointments until the people fill the vacancies by election as the legislature may direct.

This amendment shall not be so construed as to affect the election or term of any Senator chosen before it becomes valid as part of the Constitution.

Amendment XVIII

Passed by Congress December 18, 1917. Ratified January 16, 1919. Repealed by the Twenty-first Amendment.

Section 1
After one year from the ratification of this article the manufacture, sale, or transportation of intoxicating liquors within, the importation thereof into, or the exportation thereof from the United States and all territory subject to the jurisdiction thereof for beverage purposes is hereby prohibited.

Section 2
The Congress and the several States shall have concurrent power to enforce this article by appropriate legislation.

Section 3
This article shall be inoperative unless it shall have been ratified as an amendment to the Constitution by the legislatures of the several States, as provided in the Constitution, within seven years from the date of the submission hereof to the States by the Congress.

Amendment XIX

Passed by Congress June 4, 1919. Ratified August 18, 1920.

The right of citizens of the United States to vote shall not be denied or abridged by the United States or by any State on account of sex.

Congress shall have power to enforce this article by appropriate legislation.

Amendment XX

Passed by Congress March 2, 1932. Ratified January 23, 1933.

Note: Article I, Section 4, of the Constitution was modified by Section 2 of this amendment. In addition, a portion of the Twelfth Amendment was superseded by Section 3.

Section 1
The terms of the President and the Vice President shall end at noon on the 20th day of January, and the terms of Senators and Representatives at noon on the 3d day of January, of the years in which such terms would have ended if this article had not been ratified; and the terms of their successors shall then begin.

Section 2
The Congress shall assemble at least once in every year, and such meeting shall begin at noon on the 3d day of January, unless they shall by law appoint a different day.

Section 3

If, at the time fixed for the beginning of the term of the President, the President elect shall have died, the Vice President elect shall become President. If a President shall not have been chosen before the time fixed for the beginning of his term, or if the President elect shall have failed to qualify, then the Vice President elect shall act as President until a President shall have qualified; and the Congress may by law provide for the case wherein neither a President elect nor a Vice President shall have qualified, declaring who shall then act as President, or the manner in which one who is to act shall be selected, and such person shall act accordingly until a President or Vice President shall have qualified.

Section 4

The Congress may by law provide for the case of the death of any of the persons from whom the House of Representatives may choose a President whenever the right of choice shall have devolved upon them, and for the case of the death of any of the persons from whom the Senate may choose a Vice President whenever the right of choice shall have devolved upon them.

Section 5

Sections 1 and 2 shall take effect on the 15th day of October following the ratification of this article.

Section 6

This article shall be inoperative unless it shall have been ratified as an amendment to the Constitution by the legislatures of three-fourths of the several States within seven years from the date of its submission.

Amendment XXI

Passed by Congress February 20, 1933. Ratified December 5, 1933.

Section 1
The eighteenth article of amendment to the Constitution of the United States is hereby repealed.

Section 2
The transportation or importation into any State, Territory, or Possession of the United States for delivery or use therein of intoxicating liquors, in violation of the laws thereof, is hereby prohibited.

Section 3
This article shall be inoperative unless it shall have been ratified as an amendment to the Constitution by conventions in the several States, as provided in the Constitution, within seven years from the date of the submission hereof to the States by the Congress.

Amendment XXII

Passed by Congress March 21, 1947. Ratified February 27, 1951.

Section 1
No person shall be elected to the office of the President more than twice, and no person who has held the office of

President, or acted as President, for more than two years of a term to which some other person was elected President shall be elected to the office of President more than once. But this Article shall not apply to any person holding the office of President when this Article was proposed by Congress, and shall not prevent any person who may be holding the office of President, or acting as President, during the term within which this Article becomes operative from holding the office of President or acting as President during the remainder of such term.

Section 2

This article shall be inoperative unless it shall have been ratified as an amendment to the Constitution by the legislatures of three-fourths of the several States within seven years from the date of its submission to the States by the Congress.

Amendment XXIII

Passed by Congress June 16, 1960. Ratified March 29, 1961.

Section 1

The District constituting the seat of Government of the United States shall appoint in such manner as Congress may direct:

A number of electors of President and Vice President equal to the whole number of Senators and Representatives in Congress to which the District would be entitled if it were a State, but in no event more than the least populous State; they shall be in addition to those appointed by the States, but they shall be considered, for the purposes of the election of President and Vice President, to be electors appointed by a State; and they shall meet in the District and perform such duties as provided by the twelfth article of amendment.

Section 2
The Congress shall have power to enforce this article by appropriate legislation.

Amendment XXIV

Passed by Congress August 27, 1962. Ratified January 23, 1964.

Section 1
The right of citizens of the United States to vote in any primary or other election for President or Vice President, for electors for President or Vice President, or for Senator or Representative in Congress, shall not be denied or abridged by the United States or by any State by reason of failure to pay poll tax or other tax.

Section 2
The Congress shall have power to enforce this article by appropriate legislation.

Amendment XXV

Passed by Congress July 6, 1965. Ratified February 10, 1967.

Note: Article II, Section 1, of the Constitution was affected by the Twenty-fifth Amendment.

Section 1

In case of the removal of the President from office or of his death or resignation, the Vice President shall become President.

Section 2

Whenever there is a vacancy in the office of the Vice President, the President shall nominate a Vice President who shall take office upon confirmation by a majority vote of both Houses of Congress.

Section 3

Whenever the President transmits to the President pro tempore of the Senate and the Speaker of the House of Representatives his written declaration that he is unable to discharge the powers and duties of his office, and until he transmits to them a written declaration to the contrary, such powers and duties shall be discharged by the Vice President as Acting President.

Section 4

Whenever the Vice President and a majority of either the principal officers of the executive departments or of such other body as Congress may by law provide, transmit to the President pro tempore of the Senate and the Speaker of the House of Representatives their written declaration that the President is unable to discharge the powers and duties of his office, the Vice President shall immediately assume the powers and duties of the office as Acting President.

Thereafter, when the President transmits to the President pro tempore of the Senate and the Speaker of the House of Representatives his written declaration that no inability exists, he shall resume the powers and duties of his office unless the Vice President and a majority of either the principal officers of the executive department or of such other body as Congress may by law provide, transmit within four days to the President pro tempore of the Senate and the Speaker of the House of Representatives their written declaration that the President is unable to discharge the powers and duties of his office. Thereupon Congress shall decide the issue, assembling within forty-eight hours for that purpose if not in session. If the Congress, within twenty-one days after receipt of the latter written declaration, or, if Congress is not in session, within twenty-one days after Congress is required to assemble, determines by two-thirds vote of both Houses that the President is unable to discharge the powers and duties of his office, the Vice President shall continue to discharge the same as Acting President; otherwise, the President shall resume the powers and duties of his office.

Amendment XXVI

Passed by Congress March 23, 1971. Ratified July 1, 1971.

Note: Amendment XIV, Section 2, of the Constitution was modified by Section 1 of the Twenty-sixth Amendment.

Section 1
The right of citizens of the United States, who are eighteen years of age or older, to vote shall not be denied or abridged by the United States or by any State on account of age.

The Congress shall have power to enforce this article by appropriate legislation.

Amendment XXVII

Originally proposed Sept. 25, 1789. Ratified May 7, 1992.

No law, varying the compensation for the services of the Senators and Representatives, shall take effect, until an election of representatives shall have intervened.

APPENDIX C

The Emancipation Proclamation

••

January 1, 1863

By the President of the United States of America:

A Proclamation.

Whereas, on the twenty-second day of September, in the year of our Lord one thousand eight hundred and sixty-two, a proclamation was issued by the President of the United States, containing, among other things, the following, to wit:

"That on the first day of January, in the year of our Lord one thousand eight hundred and sixty-three, all persons held as slaves within any State or designated part of a State, the people whereof shall then be in rebellion against the United States, shall be then, thenceforward, and forever free; and the Executive Government of the United States, including the military and naval authority thereof, will recognize and maintain the freedom of such persons, and will do no act or acts to repress such persons, or any of them, in any efforts they may make for their actual freedom.

"That the Executive will, on the first day of January afore-said, by proclamation, designate the States and parts of States, if any, in which the people thereof, respectively, shall then be in rebellion against the United States; and the fact that any State, or the people thereof, shall on that day be, in good faith, represented in the Congress of the United States by members chosen thereto at elections wherein a majority of the qualified voters of such State shall have participated, shall, in the absence of strong countervailing testimony, be deemed conclusive evidence that such State, and the people thereof, are not then in rebellion against the United States."

Now, therefore I, Abraham Lincoln, President of the United States, by virtue of the power in me vested as Commander-in-Chief, of the Army and Navy of the United States in time of actual armed rebellion against the authority and govern-ment of the United States, and as a fit and necessary war measure for suppressing said rebellion, do, on this first day of January, in the year of our Lord one thousand eight hun-dred and sixty-three, and in accordance with my purpose so to do publicly proclaimed for the full period of one hun-dred days, from the day first above mentioned, order and designate as the States and parts of States wherein the peo-ple thereof respectively, are this day in rebellion against the United States, the following, to wit:

Arkansas, Texas, Louisiana, (except the Parishes of St. Bernard, Plaquemines, Jefferson, St. John, St. Charles, St. James Ascension, Assumption, Terrebonne, Lafourche, St. Mary, St. Martin, and Orleans, including the City of New Orleans) Mississippi, Alabama, Florida, Georgia,

South Carolina, North Carolina, and Virginia, (except the forty-eight counties designated as West Virginia, and also the counties of Berkley, Accomac, Northampton, Elizabeth City, York, Princess Ann, and Norfolk, including the cities of Norfolk and Portsmouth[)], and which excepted parts, are for the present, left precisely as if this proclamation were not issued.

And by virtue of the power, and for the purpose aforesaid, I do order and declare that all persons held as slaves within said designated States, and parts of States, are, and henceforward shall be free; and that the Executive government of the United States, including the military and naval authorities thereof, will recognize and maintain the freedom of said persons.

And I hereby enjoin upon the people so declared to be free to abstain from all violence, unless in necessary self-defence; and I recommend to them that, in all cases when allowed, they labor faithfully for reasonable wages.

And I further declare and make known, that such persons of suitable condition, will be received into the armed service of the United States to garrison forts, positions, stations, and other places, and to man vessels of all sorts in said service.

And upon this act, sincerely believed to be an act of justice, warranted by the Constitution, upon military necessity, I invoke the considerate judgment of mankind, and the gracious favor of Almighty God.

In witness whereof, I have hereunto set my hand and caused the seal of the United States to be affixed.

Done at the City of Washington, this first day of January, in the year of our Lord one thousand eight hundred and sixty three, and of the Independence of the United States of America the eighty-seventh.

By the President: ABRAHAM LINCOLN

WILLIAM H. SEWARD, Secretary of State.

Index

••

183